CREATION

of the

MODERN MIDDLE EAST

Turkey

CREATION

of the

MODERN MIDDLE EAST

CREATION

of the

MODERN MIDDLE EAST

Turkey

Second Edition

Heather Lehr Wagner | Series Editor: Arthur Goldschmidt Jr.

CHELSEA HOUSE
P U B L I S H E R S

An imprint of Infobase Publishing

Turkey, Second Edition

Copyright © 2009 by Infobase Publishing

All rights reserved. No part of this book may be reproduced or utilized in any form or by any means, electronic or mechanical, including photocopying, recording, or by any information storage or retrieval systems, without permission in writing from the publisher. For information contact:

Chelsea House
An imprint of Infobase Publishing
132 West 31st Street
New York NY 10001

Library of Congress Cataloging-in-Publication Data
Wagner, Heather Lehr.
  Turkey / by Heather Lehr Wagner. — 2nd ed.
    p. cm. — (Creation of the modern Middle East)
  Includes bibliographical references and index.
  ISBN 978-1-60413-024-9 (hardcover)
  1. Turkey—History—20th century. I. Title. II. Series.
  DR576.W34 2008
  956.1′02—dc22   2008016981

Chelsea House books are available at special discounts when purchased in bulk quantities for businesses, associations, institutions, or sales promotions. Please call our Special Sales Department in New York at
(212) 967-8800 or (800) 322-8755.

You can find Chelsea House on the World Wide Web at
http://www.chelseahouse.com

Series design by Annie O'Donnell
Cover design by Jooyoung An

Printed in the United States of America

Bang EJB 10 9 8 7 6 5 4 3 2 1

This book is printed on acid-free paper.

All links and Web addresses were checked and verified to be correct at the time of publication. Because of the dynamic nature of the Web, some addresses and links may have changed since publication and may no longer be valid.

Contents

Presidential Politics

On August 28, 2007, a 56-year-old economist named Abdullah Gül was chosen by the Turkish parliament as the new president of Turkey. Gül is an experienced politician who has served briefly as prime minister and for more than four years as foreign minister, championing the causes of democratic reform and Turkey's effort to win membership in the European Union (EU).

Despite his impressive resumé, Gül's elevation to the presidency was far from certain. In May, millions of Turks had taken to the streets, marching in protest against Gül's potential candidacy. For four months, his rise to the presidency had been blocked by much of the political establishment and, more significantly, by Turkey's powerful military, which had removed governments from power four times in the past—in 1960, 1971, 1980, and 1997. According to the BBC, the night before the final voting, the head of Turkey's armed forces, General Yaser Buyukanit, had spoken ominously of "centers of evil" trying to undermine the country.

The reason for the protests and the efforts by the military to block Gül's elevation to the presidency? Abdullah Gül is an observant Muslim with a background in Islamic politics.

From the time the Republic of Turkey was first established in 1923, it has firmly defined itself as a secular (non-religious) country. Gül's election as president represented the first time that a person with an Islamic party background had become head of state, which signified a dramatic shift in Turkey's politics.

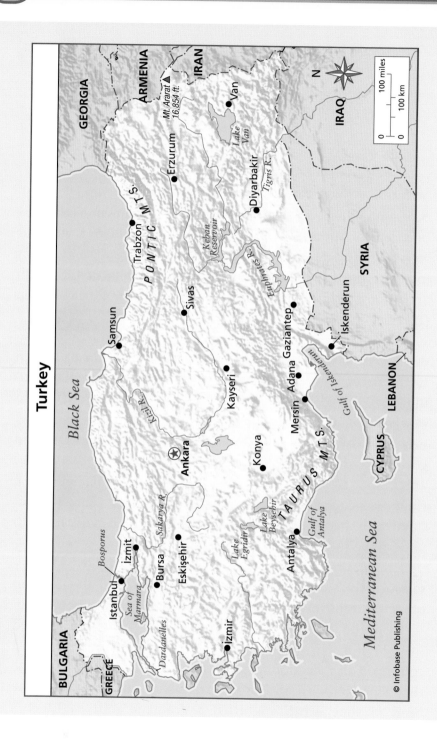

Turkey

Turkey's government is largely a parliamentary system. This means many major decisions are made by the parliament (the legislative branch), carried out by the cabinet, and ratified by the president. The head of the parliament, the prime minister, is also a powerful position, arguably more powerful than the presidency. Gül's election marked the first time since the country's founding that the presidency, prime ministership, and a majority of the seats in the parliament were all held by members of an Islamic-inspired party, in this case the Justice and Development Party, known by its Turkish initials, AK.

The AK Party (also known as AKP) held considerable power in the government since 2002, and in that time had firmly stated its commitment to Turkey's secular government, with its focus on a strict separation of church and state. Still, many in Turkey's establishment were concerned because the AK Party was a spin-off from the Welfare Party, which had been banned after its outspoken efforts to view Turkey as part of the Islamic world and its opposition to Turkish membership in the EU. Mr. Gül himself had once been a member of the Welfare Party.

Gül and other prominent members of the AK Party had worked hard in recent years to emphasize a more liberal form of politics. They had championed reforms, including judicial reforms, designed to help Turkey meet the EU's requirements for membership. Gül, one of the founders of the AK Party, had stated prior to his election that his desire was to represent all Turks. "Secularism, one of the basic principles of our Republic, is a rule of social peace," he said during his acceptance speech. "My door will be open to everyone."

(opposite) Approximately the size of Texas, Turkey's location has contributed to its economic development, largely through international trade. Influences from Eastern Europe, Central Asia, and the Middle East have merged with Islam, creating a genuinely unique culture in the region.

A SIGNIFICANT CHANGE

While Gül's religious background sparked much international concern, within Turkey people were equally concerned about his origins in Kayseri, a town in one of Turkey's more rural eastern provinces. Since the time of the country's founding, power in Turkey had resided in the hands of secular, urban leaders, most of them members of Turkey's elite class. Class divisions have long existed in Turkish society, and the people in all classes in Turkey's rural regions are generally viewed as more religious and traditional than those living in the city. Gül's election represented a shift in power to middle-class, provincial politicians—politicians generally considered more conservative than those in urban areas, although the focus of the AK Party itself has been on reform.

Opponents of Gül (and the AK Party) had focused on his Islamic background, hinting that his election would represent a step backward for the nation and an end to Turkey's efforts to win EU membership. Their arguments carried little weight because the AK Party had been in power in the parliament for four years and had made no effort to tamper with Turkey's secular tradition. In fact, the 2007 election became a referendum on the AK Party and those past four years, and voters overall confirmed their satisfaction with the party and its direction.

In April–May, when Gül's candidacy first was announced, secularist parties hinted that the AK Party had a secret Islamist agenda, which would become clear once it held not only the prime minister's post but also that of president. These parties announced their decision to boycott the vote in the parliament. The prime minister, AK Party member Recep Tayyip Erdoğan, responded by announcing a decision to hold nationwide parliamentary elections. This strategy would, in a sense, serve as the best way to gauge the popular support for an AK Party president while forcing critics to defend their own record to the voters. If members of the secular parties won a majority of seats in the parliament, the presidency would not go to Gül, but if the AK Party

Elected in 2007, Abdullah Gül *(with his wife, Hayrunnisa)* is the first Turkish president with an Islamist political past. Having previously served as the country's foreign minister, Gül has experience with being in a position that requires him to balance the needs of a democratic government, a secular society, and his own personal beliefs.

won a decisive victory, it would prove to all in Turkey that there was popular support not only for the party, but also for Gül.

The nationwide parliamentary election was held on July 22, 2007, and the result was a larger-than-expected victory for the AK Party. AK won nearly half of the votes—46.6 percent of all votes cast—while the main secular party, the Republican People's Party, received only 20.9 percent. The election denied the AK a two-thirds majority—the amount it would need to change Turkey's constitution—but it did give the party 340 seats in the 500-seat parliament. The results also gave the party the right to nominate Gül for the presidency.

Even after the parliamentary elections in July, Gül's election was far from certain. In the two initial rounds of voting in the parliament—on August 20 and 24—Gül failed to get the two-thirds votes necessary to win the presidency. But in the third round, only a simple majority (276 votes) was needed, and this Gül easily accomplished, actually winning some 330 votes. Although opposition parties had boycotted the election in the spring, blocking Gül's election because not enough legislators were present at the time of voting, few chose to boycott in August, and the opposition candidates, Sabahattin Çakmakoğlu and Hüseyin Tayfun Içli, received only 70 and 13 votes, respectively.

As president, Gül does not enjoy all the powers of an American president. His role in Turkey is more limited, although he is commander in chief of Turkey's powerful military; has veto power over legislation; and controls many important appointments, including the prime minister and members of the judicial branch. His victory has a strong symbolic meaning, as he has won the office once held by Turkey's dynamic founder, Mustafa Kemal Atatürk, a man fiercely committed to building a secular republic in the land that had once been the home to Islam's chief spiritual leader.

SIGNIFICANT STEPS

In his role as foreign minister since 2003, Gül had enjoyed a more international profile than some of his predecessors. In late 2002 and early 2003, he briefly served as prime minister during a period when some changes were made to Turkey's constitution.

Gül was born on October 10, 1950, and studied economics at Istanbul University, graduating in 1971 and later earning a Ph.D. He also studied in Great Britain, living both there and in Saudi Arabia for brief periods. He joined Turkey's parliament in 1991 as a member of the more stridently Islamic Welfare Party, and became a founding member of the AK Party in 2001.

In 1980, Gül married Hayrunnisa Ozyurt, with whom he would later have a daughter and two sons. In fact, Gül's wife became an issue of contention during the election because of her practice of wearing a head scarf. From the time of Turkey's founding, the people were actively discouraged from wearing any forms of traditional Muslim headgear as part of an effort to steer them away from their Islamic past and toward a secular and more European future. The issue is considered so fundamental that head scarves are banned from government buildings.

This attitude toward the head scarf has continued as a symbolic representation of Turkey's efforts to redefine itself as a Western nation, but years before his election to the presidency, Gül questioned its relevance in the secular/religious debate. "When my wife went to MIT in Boston," he told Stephen Kinzer, author of *Crescent and Star: Turkey Between Two Worlds*, "she wore her head scarf to class every day and nobody said a word. If an exam was scheduled on a Muslim holy day, she would ask the professor if she could take it on another day, and every professor agreed immediately. The United States is a secular country that doesn't allow religion to influence government but doesn't suppress it either. That's all we want for Turkey."

Gül's statement indicated a desire for a country where people could voice their religious beliefs without defining the state. But Turkey's efforts to carve out a strictly secular state are based on a more complicated and recent past than that of the United States. In a republic that is less than 100 years old, there is still much to remind its people of a time when the religious leader of all Muslims during the Ottoman Empire, the caliph, issued decrees from his home in the Turkish city of Istanbul. The dynamic leader who founded the Republic of Turkey, Mustafa Kemal Atatürk, had shaped a country founded on secular principles, firmly abolishing much of Turkey's Islamic past and working to create a nation more closely linked to Europe than to the Middle East.

In all these years since its founding, however, Turkey has remained poised between two different destinies, alternately embracing and shunning its past, continually rebuffed in its efforts to join the European Union but fiercely divided over whether the country's leadership should rest so firmly in the hands of former Islamists. The military hovers in the background as a constant threat to overthrow the government yet again if it senses that it is straying too far from the secular principles on which Turkey was founded.

The election of Abdullah Gül has represented a new era in Turkey's politics, a shift in power away from Turkey's elite and military and toward a middle class in the process of changing. According to a leading Turkish sociology professor quoted in the *New York Times*, "It's a very important turning point. Those people who are the peasants and farmers. . . . always had republican values imposed on them. Now they are rising against it. They are saying, 'Hey, we are here, and we want our own way.'"

The Revolution Begins

A visitor to Istanbul at the beginning of the twentieth century would have found a city whose days of glory seemed far behind it. The capital of the Ottoman Empire had served as a setting for many of the greatest civilizations the world had known. The Hittites had dominated the region during the Middle Bronze Age, fighting Egyptian pharaohs and battling the Greeks until losing the land to the Persians. Alexander the Great conquered the land around 300 B.C., and later came the mighty Roman Empire. The ancient city of Byzantium was rebuilt under Constantine in A.D. 300, and as the new capital city, it became known as Constantinople. An entire empire—the Byzantine Empire—spread out from this city into Asia and the Balkan Peninsula. Later, conquering tribes moved from the city of Mecca into the region.

By 1453, a new group had swept into Constantinople: fierce tribesmen who traveled across the lands, seizing territory as they headed west across Asia and on into Europe. Placing their capital in the same glittering setting that Constantine had chosen, the Ottomans created an empire that was the most powerful in the world in the 1500s and 1600s. This territory, known as the Ottoman Empire, spread out into Asia, parts of Europe, northern Africa, and the countries known today as Iran, Saudi Arabia, Iraq, and Syria.

The Ottoman Empire had a vast international trade network, with huge shipping and extensive caravan capacity. Relying on forced labor, the empire's economic growth also depended on its ability to continue to invade new lands, seize their goods, and capture new workers. But it became increasingly difficult to govern so many different peoples, keep so many territories in line,

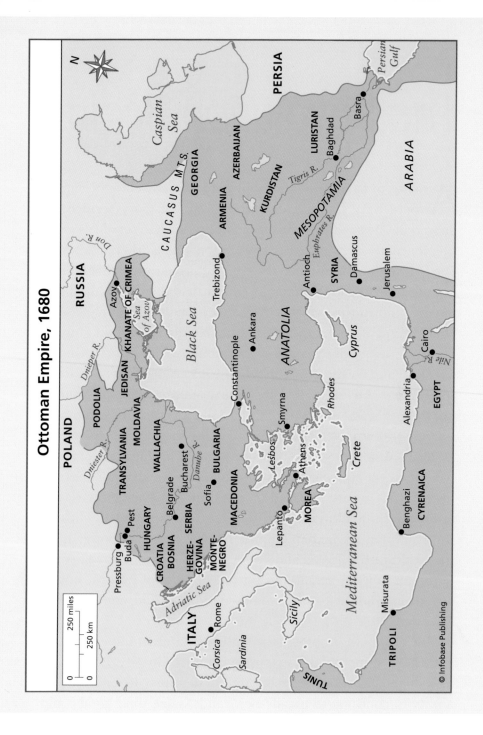

Ottoman Empire, 1680

© Infobase Publishing

and ensure that orders were followed while also conquering ever new regions.

The Ottoman Empire had known great success in medieval times (pioneering the use of firearms on land and sea), but by the seventeenth century, the European armies were becoming increasingly sophisticated as well. Developments in science and technology led to great advances in the West, advances that the Ottomans ignored or adopted too late. The Ottoman Empire had thrived as a medieval power but lost ground as it continued to cling fast to the ideas and actions that had once brought success.

Gradually, its territories slipped away. Corruption dominated the government. The sultans who ruled the empire frequently had seized the throne from family members, either by murdering them or locking them away. Citizens of the empire were divided into two general classes, or groups. The upper class, which included the imperial family, wealthy landowners, and religious and military leaders, paid no taxes. The lower class, consisting mainly of peasants, farmers, and some craftsmen, paid taxes to support the lavish lifestyles of its rulers.

Islamic rules and religion dominated the daily life of most Ottomans. The neighborhood mosque (the Muslim place of worship) was the focus of daily life—boys were educated there, social activities took place there, and representatives were selected from the mosque (as well as other places of worship) to make the people's needs known to the sultan. While Islam was the chief religion, the Ottomans did allow other religious groups to flourish, and Jews and Christians lived in relative peace with the Muslim majority.

(opposite) The Ottoman Empire was founded in the late thirteenth century and dismantled in the early twentieth century. At the height of its power (1500s to 1600s), the empire spanned three continents, controlling much of Southeastern Europe, the Middle East, and North Africa.

Inclusive Ottoman attitudes allowed Jewish and Christian influences to mix with various aspects of Islam. The Hagia Sophia *(above)*, a former Christian church in Constantinople (present-day Istanbul), inspired Muslim architects to use domes to create larger, grander mosques for their growing communities.

Women fared less well than men in the strict climate of the Ottoman Empire. A man was allowed more than one wife, and his harem (the women of the household) of as many as four wives lived in a separate section of the house, emerging in public only rarely, and then always shielded from public view by a veil.

The oppressive taxes, the frequently weak sultans, the corruption and bribery that marked the military, all contributed to the shrinking of the empire. By the beginning of the twentieth century, it had lost important territories such as Greece and Egypt. With each loss of outer territory, large groups of Muslim refugees would come pouring into the core remains of the empire. Rumblings of nationalism, first having touched the people in the farthest stretches of the empire, now echoed in the streets of the capital city.

A visitor to Istanbul in those early days of the twentieth century would find the seaport built on the seven hills still bustling with trade, but also with whispers of dissatisfaction. The lovely mosque Hagia Sophia (originally a Christian church dating back to A.D. 537), its four minarets glistening in the bright light, would still call the faithful to prayer under its impressive dome. And the palace of the Ottoman sultans still provided an awesome symbol of the power of the once-mighty empire, although the streets of the seaport now contained rumors of revolution. The plotters were young and well-connected. And the empire that had once ruled a vast stretch of the world had shrunk to a mere shadow of its former self. It was prepared to counter threats from outside forces, but the greatest threat would soon come from within.

THE YOUNG TURKS

In the early days of the twentieth century, the crumbling Ottoman Empire was ruled by the sultan Abdul Hamid. Hamid felt his power slipping away, and rather than relaxing the strength of his rule, he tightened his grip, suspending the constitution, disbanding the parliament, and using a secret police force to spy on his people and punish any who disagreed with his policies. The secret police stamped out dissidents in Istanbul, but they were less vigilant in some of the farther regions of the empire.

In the port town of Salonica (now known as Thessaloniki in a region that today belongs to Greece), the headquarters of the Ottoman 3rd Army was located, and there a secret society was formed that would forever change Turkey. The Committee of Union and Progress, or C.U.P., was born in a climate of dis-satisfaction and disorder in this area that made up one of the most important cities of the Ottoman Empire. The members of this new and secret party, many of whom came from the army, swore loyalty to only two things: the Koran (the holy book of the Islamic faith) and the gun. As the revolutionary fervor grew, the young soldiers who had joined the society in protest against the corruption they saw all around them were promoted to higher ranks within the army, and soon had weapons and men under their command. In addition, the conditions in Salonica were growing increasingly hazardous from the struggle to hold the remains of the empire together with little support from the sultan. In fact, Hamid feared a possible coup from the army and kept his soldiers begging for equipment and money, as they went months without pay and faced more frequent attacks from guerrilla groups with out-of-date weapons. These soldiers on the front lines could clearly see their portion of the empire slipping away.

Thus, when the revolution came, it began not with an oppressed group of peasants, but rather with the elite itself, young captains and majors in the army who wanted not to destroy the class system but rather to be able to fulfill their leadership roles effectively and defend their homeland against the Russians or their Orthodox Christian allies in the Balkans (southeastern Europe) in the ways in which they had been trained from an early age. They did not want to create a new nation—they wanted to restore their nation to its former glory.

By 1908, rumors of trouble had reached the sultan's ears. At first, he dismissed them. By the time he sent out spies to assess the situation, the rebellion needed only a small spark to set a revolution in motion, and the sultan provided it. One young officer named Enver Bey was thought by Hamid's spies to be at the heart of much of the trouble. He received a suspicious note from the sultan's commissioner, asking him to report to the capital city to sort out the situation and receive a promotion. Enver

Bey suspected a nasty result from his trip to Istanbul and instead escaped to the nearby hills.

Another member of the C.U.P. soon followed—Major Ahmed Niyazi—who took with him weapons, supplies, money, and 200 men. He had no intention of surrendering quietly, as is clear in a note he wrote to his brother-in-law on the night before his escape: "I see no point in lengthy explanations. The cause is known. Rather than live basely, I have preferred to die."

Niyazi did not die—he and his fellow revolutionaries escaped and gained in strength and numbers as news of the rebellion spread throughout the army. The sultan tried bribery, spying, and even harsh punishment, but all failed. On July 21, 1908, a telegram arrived at the sultan's palace from the C.U.P. It demanded that the constitution immediately be put back into effect. If not, the message warned, Hamid's heir would be proclaimed the new sultan and an army of 100,000 men would march on Istanbul. After two days of desperate searches for a way out, the sultan realized that he had no choice. On July 24, he announced that the constitution had been restored. The Young Turks (an umbrella that encompassed many groups of that time), as the revolutionaries came to be known, had won this battle. But the war was only beginning.

THE BIRTH OF A WARRIOR

Less than 30 years before the launch of the C.U.P., the town of Salonica had witnessed another birth, one that would prove equally significant in the history of the land that would become Turkey. In the winter of 1881, a young man was born to a middle-class Muslim family. In keeping with the tradition of the time of giving babies names with religious significance, he was named Mustafa, meaning "the chosen," one of the names by which the Prophet Muhammad was known in the Muslim faith. The precise date of his birth is unknown, having been recorded in a family Koran that later disappeared.

Mustafa knew tragedy early in his life. Of his six brothers and sisters, only he and a sister would survive. His father died when Mustafa was seven years old, and he moved with his mother and sister to his uncle's farm. The opportunities there for education were few, and Mustafa's mother decided to send him back to Salonica to live with relatives and attend school.

The city of Salonica, like much of the Ottoman Empire, was caught between two worlds as the nineteenth century came to a close. As European travelers and tradesmen came into the region, settling in different parts of the empire, they brought with them European ideas and progressive concepts that frequently clashed with the traditions of Islam. Salonica contained many Jews and Christians who also had a Westernizing influence. In the schools of Salonica, the conflict was clear. There were two choices for parents: They could send their children to the traditional schools whose teaching was based on the Koran or to the new system of civil and military schools operated by the state and designed to prepare children to become the government workers and military officers of the future. These state schools were considered to be more progressive and "European" than the traditional ones. In fact, Mustafa's father had fought with his mother over which school their son would attend. His father preferred the more modern state school, while his mother argued bitterly for the traditional neighborhood school.

In the end, Mustafa found himself in Salonica's state school to be prepared for a career in government. He was no model student, and after being beaten by a teacher for fighting with a classmate, he was pulled out of that school by his grandmother. The young Mustafa then wanted to attend the military academy, largely because he loved the military uniforms the students got to wear. The blonde, blue-eyed Mustafa had become vain about his appearance. The traditional Turkish costume with baggy pants and a cummerbund that students in the civil school wore seemed old-fashioned to him. His neighbor's son attended the military school, and Mustafa was jealous of his stylish uniform. He begged his mother to let him enroll in the military academy, but she was worried about the danger, uncertainty, and travel away from home a soldier's life would involve. She refused.

Nonetheless, Mustafa secretly took the entrance exams and only after he was admitted did he approach his mother with his plans. She finally relented, and so her 12-year-old son began his 13 years of military education.

The military academies of the time were training an elite class, and they took the instruction seriously. Students were educated in history, economics, and philosophy, as well as military skills. The system of teaching used at the time involved memorization. In each class, a teacher would appoint one student to serve as the "repeater," leading the class in repeating passages aloud over and over again until they had been memorized. Mustafa took on this role in the classroom, and soon became a successful student. He won sergeant stripes, became the leader of his class, and took on a second name.

He would later claim that the new last name was given to him by his math teacher, who was impressed by his skill at solving problems. That last name, Kemal, means "perfection" in Turkish. And so, at the age of 13 or 14, the future leader of Turkey became Mustafa Kemal.

By March 13, 1899, Kemal had completed military high school and entered the infantry class of Istanbul's War College. He was 18 years old. Although he and his fellow students were considered an elite group of young men, preparing to defend their sultan and their empire, they had to suffer through the "boot camp" standard for new recruits. They were treated roughly by their superior officers, fed simple food, expected to observe traditional Islamic rules for prayer five times a day, and allowed to read only textbooks.

It took him a while to find his place at the college, but Kemal settled in and became a hardworking student, earning the post of junior sergeant in charge of his class and winning special recognition for his skill in French. This training would benefit Kemal throughout his life, but an even more important benefit of his

Mustafa Kemal was a commanding military officer, leader of the Turkish revolution, and founder and first president of the Republic of Turkey. He created a modern and secular state out of the ruins of the Ottoman Empire, developing a major program of political, economic, and cultural reforms. His doctrines continue to influence the politics of Turkey today.

time at the college were the friendships he formed there, people who would become a core group that would fight together in the First World War and then go on to form the resistance movement that would lead Turkey into a brand-new age.

THE SEEDS OF REVOLUTION

The promise of great success that had once been guaranteed for those young cadets seeking a career in the military seemed less than certain at the beginning of the twentieth century. Rumors soon reached the ears of the students that military officers were not receiving their pay on time or at all. The signs of corruption were growing clear, as spies for the sultan were richly rewarded while those fighting to protect the empire were cheated out of their salaries. The forced exercise of calling out "Long live the sultan" throughout the day annoyed these officers-in-training as they wondered whether their ruler would provide for them when their schooling had ended. Kemal's expertise in French class provided him with a firm knowledge of the facts of the French Revolution, and the experiences of the brave French revolutionaries as they overthrew a tyranni-cal ruler could not help but color his perception of the world around him.

The city in which the cadets now studied, the capital city Istanbul, was really two separate communities: the neighbor-hood known as Pera, where the Christians, Greeks, Armenians, and some Jews lived and worked, and Stambul, the neighbor-hood of the Muslims. They were separated by an estuary called the Golden Horn (*halic* in Turkish). The two communities were marked not only by their faith, but also by the history they seemed to represent. Stambul looked like a medieval city, with its palaces, its domes and minarets, a community of buildings erected in the sixteenth century that were slowly crumbling into decay. Women were seldom seen in the streets, and when they were, they were always covered in black veils. The streets seemed to come fully to life only during the five times a day that the sound of the *muezzin* (a Muslim crier) rang out from the minarets, calling the faithful to prayer.

If Stambul seemed to represent the past, the community known as Pera was marked by its modernity. Wealthy merchants built palaces here in the Western style, and the stores displayed the latest goods from Europe. The streets were full of foreign tourists, and foreigners generally also ran the hotels, cafes, and shops, benefiting from the laws that excluded them from paying any taxes.

To Kemal and his friends, the city in which they lived seemed to symbolize the decay of the Ottoman Empire. They, as future soldiers, would soon be asked to defend the empire's borders from foreign invaders, but the battle seemed already to have been lost in Istanbul, where foreigners lived in wealth and comfort while the sultan's people supported the royal family with crippling taxes.

The young cadets soon decided to produce a newspaper to circulate their thoughts to like-minded students. Newspapers were forbidden at the school, and it was illegal to publish anything critical of the sultan, but the group met in secret while they were in school and continued to meet and publish their revolutionary writings after they had finished their studies. They were eventually betrayed by a friend and briefly imprisoned. The timing was terrible, as when they were arrested, the newly graduated officers were awaiting decisions about where they were to be posted. Mustafa had been hoping for a top position with one of the Ottoman armies posted in the Balkans—he would have been closer to home and in a spot where much political action was taking place. But the month-long arrest meant a shift in his status; Kemal was sent to the 5th Army, in a less desirable outpost of the empire, the city of Damascus in Syria.

Forming part of the cavalry regiment whose assignment was to police Druze tribesmen, Kemal witnessed firsthand the poor conditions and corruption that marked the Ottoman army operating in that remote region. The army was poorly supplied, with some officers lacking boots or proper gear for operating on horseback, and there was great temptation for soldiers who were owed several months' wages to steal from the marauding tribesmen. Kemal apparently refused to participate. He wanted no money but the opportunity to do the job for which he had trained—to uphold the glory of the empire, not engage in petty stealing. He was eager to try negotiation, diplomacy, and skill to deal with the tribesmen. His superior officers viewed him as interfering, and treated him with suspicion or ignored him.

The city of Damascus was a grim place for the young officer. Far from the excitement of Istanbul or the busy prosperity of his hometown, Damascus was largely untouched by modern life. Kemal began to realize that the Ottoman Empire was its own worst enemy, its soldiers corrupt and unwilling to try anything new, its lands crippled by old-fashioned Muslim ways.

Kemal managed to find a few friends who shared his views, and they formed a secret society—the Fatherland Society. As military assignments sent him to other parts of the region, he formed new groups of officers in Jaffa, Jerusalem, and Beirut with the goal of bringing about a revolution, using force if necessary. But Kemal knew that, for the revolution to truly succeed, it had to begin not in a remote outpost of the empire but closer to its heart. He left his regiment without permission, and with the help of friends was smuggled back into his hometown of Salonica. There, other friends arranged papers that granted him a medical absence, and he was able to move about the streets of Salonica, organizing a new branch of the secret society and renaming it the Fatherland and Freedom Society, with many of his old friends from military school joining him. But his unauthorized leave soon came to the attention of the authorities, and Kemal hurried back to Damascus, completing his posting there in 1907. The society he had founded in Salonica suffered in his absence, but its members soon found another outlet for their revolutionary ideals. A new group was being formed in the city, with goals and ideas quite similar to those of Kemal. Its name: the C.U.P.

AN END AND A BEGINNING

By 1907, Kemal had completed his service in Syria and, using many of his contacts, was able to arrange a posting back in Salonica. When he returned in the fall of that year, although the whispers of revolution were growing louder in the streets of his home-town, Kemal found himself very much an outsider. His posting in Damascus, away from the action, meant that the revolution had begun without him. His Fatherland Society had disappeared, and when he joined the C.U.P., which became the dominant voice of the Young Turk movement, he found that its leaders either argued with his ideas or, worse, ignored them. So it was that when the revolution finally came, Kemal's name was not among its leaders.

In the end, the Young Turks' triumph was to be short-lived. For a brief time the constitution was restored, people danced in the streets, and the young officers were cheered by enthusiastic crowds. But their plans contained little detail beyond the restoration of the constitution. The Young Turks' patriotism could not make up for a lack of political experience. As they marched under banners proclaiming phrases like "Liberty, Equality, Fraternity, Justice," they little understood the consequences these revolutionary words would have for their beloved homeland. The justice and equality they offered were for Ottomans, especially Muslims, and not for the Christians, the Jews, and the ethnic minorities in various parts of the empire. It is not surprising, then, that this revolution, rather than holding the remains of the empire together, instead caused more pieces to split away, as other groups sought their own dreams of "liberty, equality, fraternity, and justice."

Within three months, the Ottoman region of Bulgaria declared its independence. Days later, Austria seized the Ottoman provinces of Bosnia and Herzegovina, and Crete voted to unite with Greece. The Young Turks had challenged the authority of older officers in the farther regions of the empire; now they found it increasingly difficult to maintain order in their outposts. The newspapers, freed from censorship by the revolution, published complaints against the new government, criticism of its leaders, and updates on the disastrous internal policies.

Kemal, sensing the unfortunate turn of events, became a vocal critic of the Young Turks and, to get him out of the way, they sent him to North Africa on a mission. He returned to find the C.U.P. on the brink of disaster. The revolution had begun in Salonica, but Salonica was not the capital, and in Istanbul, public—and military—discontent with the new government grew out of control. On the night of April 12, 1909, troops that had been sent to ensure that the constitution was carried out instead launched a mutiny, joined quickly by teachers and students at various religious schools in the city. They marched into the parliament building, forcing the officials there to flee. Within 24 hours, the sultan had agreed to their demand to appoint a new, more conservative head of government who would follow the rules of Muslim law. Members of the C.U.P. who were found were executed; the others fled the city or went into hiding.

A FORCE FROM SALONICA

The C.U.P. members in Salonica quickly gathered together an armed force to retake Istanbul. Kemal was appointed chief of staff of one of the divisions marching on Istanbul, and he feverishly set to work planning the attack. Within a week the army had established a base just outside the city, encircling the port by land while a fleet of ships surrounded Istanbul in the water. The forces quickly re-took the city, seized the leaders of the rebellion, and hanged several of them on Galata Bridge, the main connector between Stambul and Pera.

Because the rebellion had been supported at least in part by the sultan, the C.U.P. decided that the sultan must be replaced. Parliament was reconvened, and a vote was forced.

A small group of officials was sent to the sultan's palace to deliver the bad news. Recognizing the situation as his *kismet* (the Turkish word for "fate" or "destiny"), the sultan asked whether his life would be spared. None of the officials who had been sent knew the answer. This was too much for the sultan, who called out, "May the curse of God rest on those who have caused this

When public discontent rose up and a rebellion formed against the new government, Mustafa Kemal was put in charge of a group of a small army assigned to retake Istanbul. As they marched into the city, Kemal and his men hung leaders of the rebellion from Galata Bridge *(above)*, a famous Turkish structure that connects two different areas of city.

calamity!" He was allowed to gather a few belongings, and then was escorted to the railway station, where a special train had been prepared. The news of his destination could have been no comfort to Hamid—he was to be exiled to Salonica, the very place where all his troubles had first begun.

3

An Empire at War

Although the C.U.P. had restored its power in Istanbul, it was clear that something had gone terribly wrong with its policies to allow a rebellion to flare up so quickly. Kemal thought he knew the reason. Mixing political power and military power can be a difficult task, and in Istanbul the C.U.P. had relied too heavily on enforcing its policies through military might, rather than ensuring its support in the parliament. For a party that claimed its main goal was to follow the constitution line by line, it could not ignore the importance of the parliament in creating a stronger empire. Similarly, it was important to make sure that military officers had a clear sense of their role, rather than forcing them to combine their military duties with political jobs. Many officers had struggled with the conflicting demands of protecting the empire from external threats (such as from Russia) and internal challenges from nationalists.

Three months after the successful retaking of Istanbul, the C.U.P. held its annual meeting in Salonica. Kemal made his first political speech there, arguing that expecting military officers to be both soldiers and politicians meant that they would fail at both jobs. A strong government would require both a strong military and an effective political party, he stated. His solution: Officers would have to choose—they could be politicians or military men, but not both.

This sensible argument impressed a few in the party, but it threatened many members. One young party member sent Kemal a request to discuss the ideas he had expressed at the meeting. Sensing trouble, Kemal agreed to the meeting but, when the young man arrived at his office, Kemal casually pulled a gun from a drawer and placed it on the desk. The officer made some feeble attempts at conversation before he admitted that he had been sent to kill him. A second assassination attempt occurred when Kemal was walking in the streets of Salonica late one night. He became aware of being followed, slipped into a doorway, pulled out his gun, and waited. The hired killer slowed down, but then walked past.

Having made the argument in his first speech about the wisdom of separating political and military careers, Kemal decided to withdraw from politics and focus on his own military career. He made it clear to friends and fellow officers that the C.U.P. had turned into the kind of party he felt was doomed to failure—one relying on secret meetings, plots and counterplots, and violent means to eliminate anyone who disagreed with its policies. In any case, by 1911, the Ottoman Empire was forced to turn its focus from internal political quarrels to external threats, as Germany began to flex its muscles and war loomed on the horizon. It was Italy, however, that moved first against the Ottomans, announcing its decision to seize Turkish provinces, Tripoli and later Cyrenaica in North Africa (now eastern Libya).

Moreover, Kemal knew that Austria and Russia were stirring up nationalism, or separatist tendencies, in those parts of the Balkans still under Ottoman rule. The empire could easily splinter into chaos if threats surfaced on more than one border. As Kemal was first and foremost a soldier, he set sail for Libya on October 15, 1911, determined to assist in the effort to defend the North African frontier from Italian forces.

He would never see Salonica again. Within a year, Greek armies had invaded the city where Kemal had grown up. First, they destroyed the minarets. Then, in 1917, a disastrous fire wiped out more buildings that represented Turkish life, and, by 1923, any Muslims who had clung to the city were forced out by the Greeks. The Jewish community, which had contributed much to the wealth and success of the city, survived in much smaller numbers until World War II, when the Nazis exterminated the Jews who still lived there.

Of the few traces that remain of the Ottoman community that had inhabited the city for 500 years, there is one clue to Salonica's important role in establishing modern Turkey. Amid the concrete apartments that line the streets, you can find a heavily guarded pink wooden house, where Kemal had lived with his mother. A plaque in front explains that this is the former home of the founder of the Turkish republic.

AN EMPIRE TORN APART

The war that began on September 29, 1911, when Italian troops marched into Tripoli would involve the region in bloodshed for nearly 12 years. For one year, Kemal fought bravely in Cyrenaica against the Italian forces. By the time he returned to Istanbul in November 1912, the capital was in chaos. Students demonstrated in the streets outside the palace. As a result of the first Balkan War (1912), the region of Macedonia had been lost; Bulgaria and Serbia had fought for—and won—their autonomy; and Greek forces were massing on the Turkish border. When the Balkan forces marched into parts of European Turkey, Muslim communities fled in terror, joining the retreating Ottoman armies rather than exposing themselves to the massacres that had already been inflicted on 12,000 Muslims in Kosovo and other regions by victorious Serbian forces.

In 1913, the 32-year-old Kemal was confronted with evidence that his dreams of glory had amounted to little. He had enjoyed only small success in his military career and none at all in his political efforts. His hometown was lost to Greece, and his mother and sister were refugees, forced to flee their home. His country was dissolving. His enemies were still active.

Kemal was given the post of military attaché to the new Balkan state of Bulgaria. While the C.U.P. struggled to keep control over its capital by installing a military dictatorship, which would prove even more oppressive and corrupt than the government it had been formed to overthrow, Kemal was sent into exile in Sofia, the capital of Bulgaria.

The posting provided Kemal with his first lengthy exposure to Western life. The newly independent region was reveling in the outcome of the Balkan War, which had greatly benefited Bulgaria. Parties and balls were held everywhere, the opera gave frequent, glittering performances, and the people wore fashionable clothing they had purchased in Vienna. The Bulgarians were gracious and hospitable to the Turks they had fought only a short time before, and Kemal was a frequent guest at the wealthy homes in the city.

He toured the Turkish community in Sofia, and was amazed at the advantages Turks living there experienced over those back in Istanbul. They operated successful businesses—something that only foreigners did in the Ottoman Empire. They were wealthy. Their women were not required to be veiled. Their children were educated in modern schools.

The freedom and prosperity he saw in Sofia greatly impressed Kemal. It soon became clear that the Turkish community was enjoying a superior life here, in the territory that was once part of the Ottoman Empire, to that in Turkey itself. In those days and nights, moving among the glittering diplomats in the newly independent region, Kemal began to form plans for a modern Turkey, modeled on the Western style he saw in the streets of Sofia.

Meanwhile, back in Istanbul, the C.U.P. leadership had undertaken a series of reforms designed to shake up the army in the wake of the defeat in the Balkan Wars and invited a team of experts from Germany to assist. Ottoman military academies soon had German instructors training the future elite of the empire. German officers were added to the various army units. Turkish troops were overseen by a German military corps.

This was a policy that spelled disaster for the Ottoman Empire, for the year was 1914, and on June 28, the Archduke Ferdinand of the dual monarchy Austria-Hungary was assassinated in Sarajevo. Within a month, World War I had begun. Kemal, from his post in Sofia, argued strongly about the dangers of siding with Germany in the war. If Germany won, Turkey would become essentially its province, and if it lost, the Ottoman Empire would disappear. But his superiors disagreed (mainly because Russia, the empire's historic enemy, was allied with Great Britain and France), and by the end of October a Turkish vessel, with German officers and crew on board, sailed into the Black Sea and, without warning, attacked three Russian port cities. Russia and its allies proceeded to declare war on the Ottoman Empire.

THE BATTLE AT GALLIPOLI

Although opposed to the alliance with Germany, Kemal was eager to play a more important military role once war had been declared. After repeatedly requesting a posting on the front lines, he was ordered to return to Istanbul to assume the command of the Ottoman Empire's 19th Division. He packed quickly and left Sofia on January 20, 1915.

By the time Kemal returned to the capital, the Ottoman army had suffered two disastrous defeats, by the Russians in Eastern Anatolia and by British troops stationed at Egypt's Suez Canal. The army command seemed confused, and Kemal's experience when he arrived in Istanbul gave him ample cause for concern. He met with several officers about his new posting, but no one was able to tell him the current location of the 19th Division he was to command or whether it even existed. It was finally suggested that he might try the 3rd Army Corps, stationed at Gallipoli, south of Istanbul, where there might be plans to form such a division.

The battle for the Gallipoli Peninsula would prove to be one of the most critical of World War I. The region was strategically significant, serving as an important buffer between the Aegean Sea and Istanbul. If an invading force was able to sweep across Gallipoli and into Istanbul, the Ottoman Empire would be cut off from its German allies. The capital, Istanbul, would fall into enemy hands; Russia would be able to gain access (by sea) to territories like the Bosporus and Dardanelles straits; and Europe would be opened to attack from the south.

During World War I, British forces hoped to advance on the German and Turkish armies by invading the Ottoman Empire at Gallipoli Peninsula. Intent on conquering the area and then moving on to Istanbul, the British settled into the area for a battle *(above)*, but underestimated the strength and resolve of Mustafa Kemal and his soldiers.

Information came to the Ottomans and Germans that the British were massing troops in Egypt in preparation for an attack at Gallipoli. The British Empire forces numbered 80,000 men and the Germans and Ottomans had only 20,000 men to defend the mountainous, 52-mile-long coastline. The German command decided to break its forces into three groups, guarding the northern, southern, and central portions of the peninsula. The plan was for the smaller forces to do their best to hold off the invasion for the two or three days it would take until reinforcements could arrive. Kemal and his troops (one Turkish and two Arab regiments) were dispatched to Maidos, toward the central section of Gallipoli, and ordered to perform drills until they received word of where the British attack would occur.

On the morning of April 25, 1915, Kemal sent his strongest regiment out at 5:30 A.M. to practice maneuvers up one slope of the hillside at Chunuk Bair. The terrain was quite rough, and Kemal, moving ahead of his troops, was forced to dismount from his horse and climb the hill on foot. As he and a few officers moved up the hill, they saw a company of soldiers racing back down toward them. When Kemal shouted at them, asking why they were running, they screamed, "They come, they come."

Kemal reached the top of the hill and saw below him a line of Australian solders moving up the hill. They were closer to him than his own troops. He ordered the retreating lookouts to turn, fix their bayonets, and prepare to fight.

The Germans had believed that the strongest British attack would come at the northern part of Gallipoli. They were wrong: Kemal, with his small regiment, was facing the bulk of the invading force. Finally, his soldiers, panting from the steep climb up the hill and believing that they were at the end of their drill, joined him.

Fortunately, the regiment had prepared for the training exercise with real, rather than fake, firepower. With no time to wait for instructions from the German high command, Kemal ordered his troops to fight.

The battle raged all day and into the night. The Australians were unable to advance, but neither did they retreat back down the hill. Each side dug in, and the fighting continued for weeks, with all suffering heavy losses. Reinforcements arrived for both sides, but the Germans remained cautious, unwilling to send a significant portion of troops anywhere for fear the British would attack the peninsula at another point and move on to Istanbul.

On three separate occasions over the next several long, hot months, Allied forces attempted to take the peninsula. In three fierce battles and many bloody skirmishes, Kemal and his troops stood their ground. Finally, in December 1915, the Allies gave up and withdrew from the peninsula. Kemal and his troops had held on and Istanbul was safe.

A FORGOTTEN HERO

When Kemal returned to Istanbul, having played this critical role at Gallipoli, there were parades to salute the victorious Ottoman forces, but it was the sultan who was cheered as the *Ghazi* (victorious warrior) and the C.U.P. leaders and senior generals who stood high on the royal platform overlooking the parade. Kemal's achievements in saving Istanbul were overlooked, his name was omitted from official decrees honoring the soldiers, and he was largely ignored upon his return to the capital.

It must have been a bitter moment for the ambitious commander whose troops had held off the invading force for so many months. Kemal lingered in the capital for only a few weeks for a much-needed sick leave before being dispatched to eastern Turkey, eastern Anatolia to be exact, to lead a corps defending the empire against an advancing Russian army. This region had been occupied by Armenians for many centuries before the Turks arrived as conquerors. The C.U.P. government had recently forced all the Armenian citizens to leave, based on a suspicion, with some basis, that they were secretly helping the Russian forces.

At the time World War I began, approximately 2 million Armenians were living in the Ottoman Empire. They were proud of their culture and heritage. The Armenian nation was the first to make Christianity its state religion, and throughout their history as a conquered people they were viewed as ideal citizens—loyal and hardworking.

With the rise to power of the Young Turks, however, the Armenians were subjected to intense discrimination. Although the Armenians managed much of the trade and were often better educated than their Turkish neighbors, the differences in religious beliefs, class, and status sparked resentment, and anti-Armenian violence soon followed.

With only trouble and no support coming from the government, the Armenians took their cause to London, Paris, Geneva, and even to the hated enemies of the Turkish people—the Russians. They began promoting their own demands for independence as well as publicizing the violent discrimination they had experienced. Their connection to the Russians seemed to threaten Turkey's security.

This would have disastrous consequences. As World War I broke out, the C.U.P. held a series of meetings calling for the removal of the Armenian population to a different location, stating their concerns about foreign influences—particularly Russian—during a time of war. What followed, from mid-June to late August of 1915, was a tragic series of violent actions. First, Armenian men were ordered to report to a central location, where they were briefly jailed and then shot. Next, the women, elderly, and children were ordered to march, carrying a few possessions, for hundreds of miles, heading for the desert or the mountains. Many died along the route from thirst, hunger, exhaustion, or exposure. As the routes of these marches were followed over and over again, later victims would encounter the unburied bodies of those who had preceded them.

In that summer of 1915, approximately one million Armenians were killed. More than half of them were women and children.

The removal of this large group of citizens left the region bleak and scarred by violence. To add to this catastrophe, hundreds of thousands of Muslim refugees, many of them Kurds, soon raced into the region, fleeing the armies of invading Russians. By the time Kemal arrived, the streets were empty of businesses and instead filled with desperate Kurd refugees looking for food. The bitter winter that followed made matters worse, as the Ottoman troops faced brutal conditions without the proper clothing or supplies. It was becoming clear that the Ottomans were fighting a losing battle.

Kemal would go on to lead troops in other parts of the empire and at the end of the war desperately attempted to hold off British forces in Palestine (the land known today as Israel). In the fall of 1918, as the war was ending, he led a well-organized

Believing the Armenians to be a threat to their security, the Turkish government organized plans to minimize the Armenian population within the empire. After removing the Armenians from their homes, some were quickly executed while others were forced to endure a brutal journey into the desert. Those who survived lived in refugee camps like the one above.

retreat of Ottoman forces from Palestine and Syria. On October 30, 1918, an armistice was signed between the Ottoman Empire and its Allied foes. Commonly called the Mudros Armistice, it provided for an Allied occupation of Istanbul and the straits. Part of the empire had been lost, and a huge number of soldiers gave up their lives. The C.U.P.'s main leaders, including many of those who had engineered the disastrous entry into the war, fled for Berlin.

Sultan Mehmet VI formed a new government without the C.U.P., but it would merely oversee the end of the empire. Ottoman hopes that signing an armistice would mean the removal of the Allied armies were quickly shattered. British troops moved in to occupy Mosul in the portion of the empire now known as Iraq. Kemal's forces in Syria were greeted with the news that British troops would soon be moving in to occupy their territory. Kemal asked if he could form small battalions to resist the invasion but instead was ordered back to Istanbul. He returned to the capital to the depressing sight of 55 Allied warships dropping anchor in the harbor outside the sultan's palace.

AN END AND A BEGINNING

For the next several months, Kemal witnessed the oppressive reality of enemy troops occupying the once-glittering capital. The Ottoman Empire had been shattered into pieces and had lost Syria, Palestine, Egypt, and Arabia. All that was left was Turkey, and it was suffering at the hands of its invaders. The sultan dissolved the parliament and, determined that his best chance of saving himself and Turkey lay in cooperation, immediately agreed to all the demands of the Allied forces. This seemed to many Turkish nationalists like capitulation.

Kemal watched in despair as his country struggled under foreign control. Then the British, learning of resistance in outposts in Anatolia, suspected that Kemal was involved and wanted to arrest him. At the same time, the sultan realized that the small rebellions could not go unchecked and proposed sending Kemal as his representative to put them down, bring a halt to gatherings of the C.U.P., and ensure that any remaining troops were disbanded. For several days, the British and the sultan argued back and forth—should Kemal be arrested for his suspected role in the rebellions in Anatolia or be sent to put a stop to them? Finally, the decision was made. The sultan refused to arrest Kemal and appointed him Inspector-General of the Northern Area and Governor-General of the Eastern Provinces.

In 1919, Kemal left immediately with a few of his closest friends. As they traveled north, they learned that the Allies had agreed to allow Greece to occupy Smyrna (now Izmir) in Turkey. It was clear that, without quick action, their homeland would disappear into small provinces divided among the victorious Allied forces. Kemal and his men determined that resistance, not cooperation, was the answer. Somehow, their decision reached the sultan, who quickly sent word to the British that he had made a mistake in promoting Kemal but he was too late to stop him before he reached his assigned post. Kemal escaped the forces sent after him only by hours.

In Anatolia, he set to work organizing pockets of resistance. He gathered together as many of the former army corps commanders as he could find. Now unemployed, these officers were quick to join Kemal's team. He went from village to village, preaching the need for resistance to the English, explaining that they could no longer rely on the sultan to protect them, that they must begin to rely on themselves. He helped organize local towns and villages to enlist volunteers.

(opposite) Ottoman fortunes began to decline after the death of Suleyman I, under whose reign the empire reached its highest point of power and splendor. By the early 1900s it controlled only the Anatolia region of present-day Turkey and parts of the Balkans and the Middle East, and lost even more territory during World War I (1914–1918).

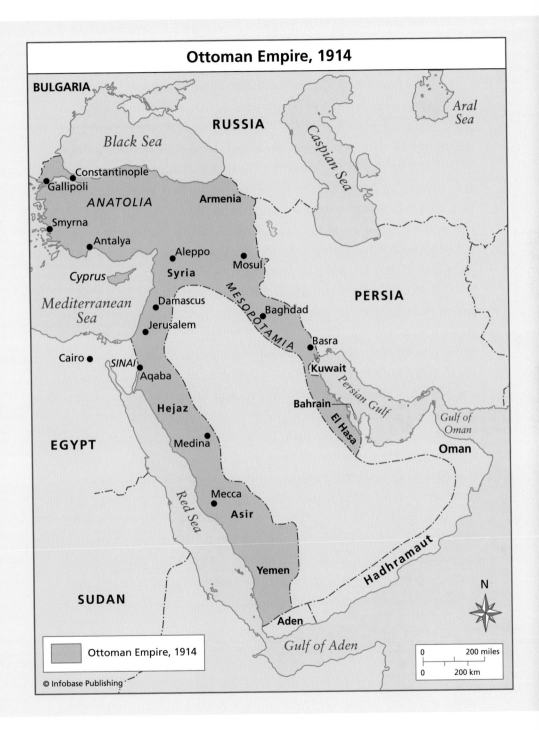

Ottoman Empire, 1914

BULGARIA

RUSSIA

Aral Sea

Black Sea

Caspian Sea

● Constantinople
Gallipoli ●

ANATOLIA

Armenia

Smyrna ●

● Antalya

● Aleppo

Mosul ●

Syria

Cyprus

PERSIA

Mediterranean Sea

● Damascus

MESOPOTAMIA

Baghdad ●

Jerusalem ●

Basra ●

Cairo ●

SINAI

Kuwait

Aqaba ●

Bahrain ●

Persian Gulf

Hejaz

El Hasa

Gulf of Oman

EGYPT

● Medina

Oman

Red Sea

Mecca ●

Asir

Hadhramaut

Yemen

N

SUDAN

Aden ●

Gulf of Aden

Ottoman Empire, 1914

| 0 | 200 miles |
| 0 | 200 km |

© Infobase Publishing

The sultan ordered him back to Istanbul, but Kemal refused to return to the capital. The sultan immediately discharged him, and Kemal in turn resigned from his army post.

He was now free to act as a civilian, and act he did. His campaign expanded from a military to a political one and gathered together a congress of delegates to lay out plans for a national government, independent of Istanbul. Kemal's opening speech before the crowd made clear his plans for Turkey: A revolution was needed to focus on the rights of the nation and the will of its people. It would create a government based on the rights of the majority, not an elite few. It was to be a government of the people and for the people, based on the principles of Western democracy that Kemal had studied for many years.

The sultan next dismissed the old government and called for new elections, in which members of the congress Kemal had formed won the majority of the votes. As the newly elected members of the parliament, they moved to Istanbul to serve their aims within the capital—all but Kemal, who distrusted the sultan and felt that revolution, not cooperation, was necessary. The British, tired of the resistance they were meeting throughout the Turkish countryside, massed around the capital for a single show of force. They marched into Istanbul, occupied the city, and arrested as many members of the parliament as they could find. The sultan stood behind British actions, and now, using his position as the head of the Muslim faith as well as the royal leader of the nation, ordered his priests to preach messages of cooperation and support rather than revolt. From town to town and village to village, government officials and religious leaders encouraged the local citizens to support their sultan, while Kemal and his fellow "nationalists," as they were now being called, spoke passionately of the need for a strong, independent Turkey, without foreign intervention.

The result was not surprising. The country split in two, and a bitter civil war began with divisions drawn between neighbors and sometimes even between members of the same family. The sultan issued a royal decree that was sent throughout the countryside. Mustafa Kemal was an outlaw, the decree stated. He must be found and killed. Whoever did so would be performing a holy duty and would be richly rewarded.

Birth of a Nation

4

For months, the fighting raged throughout the country. Quickly, foreign forces took advantage of the chaos to move in and make their own claims for territory. The Greeks moved in from their base in Smyrna (encouraged, the Turks believed, by the British prime minister David Lloyd George). The French seized land in the south. The Kurds revolted in the east.

And then came the San Remo Conference. From April 19 to 26, 1920, representatives from the Allied forces gathered together to determine how they would divide up the Ottoman Empire. The result was the Treaty of Sèvres, a document designed by the victorious Allies supposedly to formalize the peace terms agreed upon for the region, but which actually divided the empire among its conquerors into series of tiny states managed by Europeans. The lost territories would include the Arabian regions to be given to the British and French; Thrace and eight Turkish islands in the Aegean to the Greeks; and the Dodecanese Islands to Italy. Most of Anatolia would be divided into French and Italian territories. Much of Armenia would be granted its independence. The Kurds would be granted autonomy in their eastern portion of the empire. The waterways—the keys to Turkey's trade and financial survival—would be placed under Allied control. The Turkish army would be reduced to a small force overseen by the Allies, and the Turkish police would be placed under foreign control.

The response from the people was immediate—this document would mean the end of their nation, and they rejected it. The small pockets of rebels who had supported Kemal in his calls for independence quickly swelled in numbers as more and more outraged citizens joined them. The Allies decided that the nationalist forces must be wiped out, and authorized the Greek armies to march east and north to stamp out any Ottoman troops resisting the planned partition. Of all the European forces, the Greeks were the ones most hated by the Turkish people, a hatred based in history, politics, and religion. The Allies could not have made a more unfortunate choice to police their new agreement, as the sight of Greek soldiers marching into their towns would virtually guarantee that the Turkish people would rise up in protest.

At first the Greek invaders, backed by the Allies and superior to the Turkish nationalists in numbers and weaponry, advanced rapidly and widely. But then Kemal turned for help to an unlikely source—Russia. The Turks and Russians had fought each other at least once a generation for centuries, most recently during World War I. But the Russians viewed the revolutionary movement in Turkey as an extension of their own recent revolution, and they publicly supported the efforts of Kemal and his fellow nationalists. Kemal sent a delegation to this new government, requesting Russian support and supplies. The request was granted.

Aided by fresh supplies, the Turk forces gained in strength just at a point when the Greeks were weakened by the loss of support of a public grown weary of wars. By late 1922, the tide had turned and the Turkish armies were pushing Greek forces back across the territory they had seized a short time before. Only the British were left and finally they, too, agreed to restore independence in Istanbul.

On November 1, 1922, the National Assembly passed a resolution stating that the system of government based on rule by a member of the royal family had ended on March 16, 1920 (two and a half years earlier). The resolution also stated that the role of caliph (the spiritual head of Islam) should belong to a member of the royal Ottoman family, but that the Assembly would choose which member of that sovereign family had the necessary "learning and character" to best qualify him for the position.

Turkish crowds celebrate the victory of Smyrna (modern Izmir) in 1923. Smyrna came under the custody of Greece after World War I by the Treaty of Sèvres and was reclaimed and seized by the Turks, who were given its custody by the Treaty of Lausanne.

Sultan Mehmet VI did not wait for the Assembly to decide whether or not his learning and character qualified him to serve as caliph. Fearing for his life, a mere 11 days after the resolution passed, the sultan fled his palace and boarded a British warship bound for Malta. His cousin, Abdul Mejid, was named as the new caliph. Never again would a member of the Ottoman royal family rule over Turkey, and the family would not perform the function of caliph for much longer, either.

After long and often difficult negotiations between the British and the Turks, the Treaty of Lausanne was signed on July 24, 1923. It restored nearly all of the lands that make up modern Turkey to this day. It removed the hated "peace" terms that had sparked the revolution. More important, it officially agreed to the demands Kemal and his fellow nationalists had made, both military and political. It was a victory for Kemal, and yet there was one final matter to be settled before he could set to work rebuilding the nation: The Allies had invited two official groups from Turkey to participate in the official signing of the Treaty of Lausanne—the nationalists and the government of the sultan.

The nationalists had a clear plan for the future of their country—one that involved economic and scientific efforts to ensure Turkey's place as an equal in the community of nations. It was a time for strong leadership, under a single leader with a clear vision. Kemal was determined to be that leader.

The solution seemed clear. The sultan had traditionally played two key roles: He had served as both the political leader of his nation and as caliph, the religious leader of the Muslim faith, thought to be a descendant of the Prophet Muhammad himself. Kemal wanted the national leadership for himself. The sultan could, however, retain the role of caliph and carry on as spiritual leader for his people.

Less than two years after assuming the office of caliph, Abdul Mejid was awakened by frightened servants who informed him that Istanbul's governor and chief of police had come to his palace. He was told that the Grand National Assembly had met only a few hours earlier and had voted to put an end to his position as Turkey's religious leader and ordered all members of the Ottoman royal family out of the country. From now on, there would no longer be a caliph. Mejid was told to leave the palace immediately.

A furious Mejid refused to go quietly. He ordered the governor to leave the palace at once. The police chief then informed the caliph that the palace was surrounded, the phone lines had been cut off, and the police had been given the authority to remove him by force, if necessary.

Mejid had little choice but to obey. He was told that he and his family would be taken to the main train station in Istanbul and put on the Orient Express, a train bound for Europe. Mejid pleaded to be allowed to gather a few belongings, a request that was finally granted. Then, with two of his four wives, his son and daughter, and three staff members, he left the palace under police guard. Fearing that there might be trouble if the caliph was paraded through the streets of the densely populated city of Istanbul, the police decided to take Mejid and his family instead to Çatalca, a smaller train station outside the city. There, the heavily guarded group waited all day and into the night until at last, near midnight, the Orient Express pulled into the station. A private coach had been attached to the train. After boarding the coach, Mejid was given an envelope containing £2,000 in British currency as well as temporary papers entitling him to travel to Switzerland. In return, he agreed to sign a statement indicating that he was resigning as caliph to comply with the people's wishes, and would spend his remaining years studying art.

Mejid's resignation lasted for as long as it took the train to cross over the border into Bulgaria. He then immediately issued a new statement, explaining that he had resigned only under pressure, and that he considered the Assembly's decision to be invalid. But he would learn, to his astonishment, that very few people cared. It had been widely believed that almost all Muslims revered the Ottoman family and assumed that it was entitled to the caliphate, but now the world learned otherwise. The caliph endured one final indignity in his hasty flight from the country his family had ruled for centuries. When the train reached the Swiss border, Mejid was held at the frontier. A Swiss law prevented immigrants with more than one wife from entering the country. It was only after a delay that he was permitted to enter his new homeland.

The remaining members of the Ottoman royal family quickly followed Mejid into exile. Only a few days later, 116 members of the dynasty were forced to leave their homes. The majority of them would never return.

A MODERN WOMAN

In the spring of 1923, Mustafa Kemal was beginning to take the steps that would transform Turkey into a modern nation. In the Western countries he had visited, he had been impressed by the freedom women enjoyed and by the contributions they in turn made to their nations. He resolved that in a modern Turkey women would enjoy many of the same freedoms as men, no longer being segregated in their homes and in the streets. One young woman named Latife Hanim, who was working as his secretary, had made a particularly strong impression on the new leader. She came from a prosperous merchant family, spoke French fluently, and had studied law in Europe.

Kemal proposed to Latife, and she quickly accepted. The wedding symbolized the kind of modern relationship Kemal hoped for. In traditional Muslim weddings, the bride and groom do not see each other until after the ceremony, which is performed by representatives for each side. At their wedding, Kemal and Latife were married at her father's home, seated side by side at a table as they spoke their vows. In another break with tradition, Latife's face was not veiled.

For their honeymoon, Kemal took Latife on a tour of southern Anatolia. It was more a political tour than a romantic interlude. They traveled through major cities, and Latife appeared in public at Kemal's side (rather than in the harem—the part of the house set aside for women—as tradition would have dictated). She gradually began appearing without the veil, at first sparking shock, particularly in rural regions, but gradually inspiring many other Turkish women to follow her example.

Kemal emphasized, on this political campaign, not only his wife's equal status with him, but his equal status with his people. He mixed with the people, avoiding wherever possible any elaborate and formal ceremonies. In one instance, golden thrones were provided for Kemal and Latife to observe a fireworks display. He sent them away, requesting ordinary chairs placed within the crowd of people who had gathered.

Kemal's plans called for a complete break with the Ottoman Empire, with its elaborate ceremonies and strict separation of elite classes and everyday citizens. Kemal's vision for his country was of a republic whose government belonged to the people and whose national assembly would serve as the people's representatives (although political rivals soon learned that this was more talk than action when they tried to form an opposition party). It was a radical idea for a nation that had known centuries of royal rule. No more would the people's fate be left in the hands of a sultan or caliph. They would govern themselves through that national assembly and through a president elected by the assembly.

The first step toward this new national identity required a new base for the government, removed geographically and symbolically from the old capital of the sultan. On October 13, 1923, the constitution was amended to establish the capital of the Turkish state at Ankara, not Istanbul. Ankara was located in the very heart of Turkey, with none of the links to the sultans of centuries past that marked the streets of Istanbul, and was a far more primitive place than the glittering capital had been.

But a more radical change would come only a few days later, for based in the new capital city would be a brand-new form of government. On October 29, 1923, the news was proclaimed, following approval by the Assembly, that Turkey would become a republic. Its new president, elected unanimously by 158 votes in the Assembly, was Mustafa Kemal.

NEW LAWS FOR A NEW REPUBLIC

During the next few years, Mustafa Kemal began a series of radical reforms that would sweep away the vestiges of Ottoman tradition and replace them with modern planning. The first involved removing the last trace of the Ottoman royal family by abolishing the need for a caliph. No more would there be confusion about whose policies would dictate life in Turkey. Next, the separate religious schools and colleges were closed, followed by the closure of the courts in which judges trained in Islamic law (or *Sheriat*, Turkish for Sharia law) had ruled on legal matters based on their interpretations of the Koran.

Kemal had become expert in the art of revolution, first carrying out a military revolution and then a political one. But now, as president, he began a series of symbolic revolutions designed to transform Turkey into a contemporary society. Kemal believed in outward symbols as well as internal ones and so he turned to transforming his people into a modern society. Not only did he work at instilling new thoughts and beliefs, but at changing people's looks externally, through their clothing. Specifically, he changed their hats.

For 100 years, Muslim men in Turkey were identified by the *fez*, a tall, red, cylinder-shaped hat adorned with a black tassel. The shape and design was important, since it allowed Muslims to touch their foreheads to the ground in prayer, as required by their faith. It also told the knowledgeable observer something about the rank and profession of the wearer (fez wearers were normally government officials or army officers).

The fez was outlawed on November 25, 1925. Men were required to wear Western-style hats; anyone wearing a fez could be arrested. Shortly thereafter, women were discouraged from wearing the veil. Women in cities soon stopped covering their faces, although in more remote regions they continued to wear the veil. Public employees were required to wear suits made by local merchants from local cloth, and school uniforms in Western style were also regulated.

From clothing, the reforms moved on to the way Turks measured time. In a radical step for a Muslim country, the Gregorian calendar was introduced, using dates based on the Christian system of measuring time before and after Christ's death using

B.C. and A.D., as well as the 24-hour measurement of daily time popular in Europe, which starts at midnight, as opposed to the Muslim system of measuring time from the sunset. Kemal also championed a sweeping set of educational reforms, bringing in the noted educational pioneer John Dewey as a consultant.

The speed of these transformations was truly remarkable. The modern society that Kemal envisioned rapidly became a reality—it is difficult to imagine how quickly life changed for the Turkish people. Pulling a nation back from the threat of political extinction is a brilliant feat; changing the way its people think about themselves and their culture is almost impossible. And yet Kemal was able to achieve both.

Next, Kemal began his transformation of the role of women in Turkish society. For centuries, women had enjoyed little freedom in the Ottoman world. In Istanbul, a woman was forbidden from walking in the street or driving in a carriage with a man, even if he was her husband. If husband and wife went outside together, the husband had to walk several steps ahead of his wife, ignoring her. Nor did men and women go out together socially. On boats and trains there were separate sections for men and women, divided by a curtain. In the theater, Muslim women were forbidden to act in plays—the female parts were played by men. Women could only attend the theater on special "ladies' days" when the audience was reserved solely for them.

By early 1926, Kemal had overseen a further step in his platform of increased rights for women. Divorces would no longer be granted simply because the husband wished to end the marriage. Polygamy (marriage to more than one woman) was outlawed. New inheritance laws ensured that women would receive as much as men, changing the old Muslim law that dictated that female heirs could receive only half as much as their brothers did. In the past, women could only teach in all-girls schools; now they were allowed to teach in all elementary and middle schools. Women could now pursue careers in medicine and law. And, in a controversial challenge to the religious establishment and to Islamic law, Muslim women were now legally allowed to

This 1979 painting called *A Man of Action* illustrates the Turkish society's reaction to Mustafa Kemal Atatürk's laws calling for the westernizing of Turkish culture. Atatürk *(inset)* prohibited men from wearing the traditional Turkish fez and required government employees to wear suits to work. Later considered surprisingly successful, his reforms have made Turkey into one of the most progressive Muslim countries in the world.

marry non-Muslim men, and all adults were legally granted the right to change their religion if they wished to do so.

These laws represented a significant break with the past. They were a remarkable set of changes, and these swift ends to long-established customs were not always popular. But as Kemal himself said, "The civilized world is far ahead of us. We have no choice but to catch up."

It is ironic that Kemal, recognized as a champion of rights for women in Turkey, was less successful at his own efforts to maintain the modern marriage that had been an early symbol of the new society he planned. His marriage with Latife lasted only three years. Although both Kemal and Latife seemed to be models of the new roles for men and women in a modern Turkey, they were caught in the same struggles that would grip Turkey as it adapted to a changed society. Latife viewed herself as a partner, an equal, yet was unhappy and jealous when Kemal's social and political gatherings expanded to include women as well as men. Kemal, in turn, as leader of the new republic, also wanted to be leader in his own home. The clash was inevitable. Kemal ended the marriage before the new laws benefiting women went into effect. Their wedding ceremony had been done in the Western manner, but their divorce followed the Muslim tradition. Kemal simply said, "Leave the house. I do not wish to see you any more," and the marriage was legally ended.

REFLECTION AND REFORM

By 1927, Turkey's transformation was firmly underway, and a new round of elections in August and September of that year brought victory for Kemal's Republican People's Party (which he had founded in 1923). He was reelected president, and shortly after the election delivered a momentous speech that has become an important document of modern Turkish history. Known simply as the *nutuk* ("speech" in Turkish), it is a history—Kemal's history—of the birth of modern Turkey. Step-by-step, it is a retelling of Kemal's story from the moment when he landed at Samsun on May 19, 1919, to start his War of Independence. The speech took 36 hours to deliver, stretched over six separate gatherings from October 15 to 20. It ended with a stirring call to the young people of Turkey, urging them to defend the Republic and its independence, no matter what. This portion of the speech, to this day, must be memorized by all Turkish schoolchildren.

The role of religion was further diminished in Turkey with an amendment to the constitution. In the first Ottoman constitution of 1876, the words "The religion of the Turkish state is Islam" had underscored the critical importance of Muslim thought and laws, but on April 10, 1928, a law was passed which removed that phrase. The act didn't guarantee freedom of religion but defined Turkey's laws and government as secular rather than religious.

There was one additional reform Kemal needed to make to ensure that Turkey would be more closely connected to its neighbors in Western Europe than those in the east. Turkey's alphabet was Arabic with 28 letters, quite different from the Latin alphabet with 26 letters that is used in Western languages. By August of 1928, a new alphabet had been created, based on Latin rather than Arabic letters. Kemal then set out on a tour of the country, meeting people in schoolrooms, town halls, and cafes, to stress the importance of learning to read and write using this modified alphabet. On November 3, a law was passed making it illegal to use the Arabic alphabet after the end of the year.

This is another remarkable example of the changes Turkey experienced under the leadership of Mustafa Kemal. Imagine what it would have been like to live during that time, when so much of what was familiar was disappearing. The way you dressed, the alphabet you used to read and write, even the clocks and calendars used to measure time, all changed. With his vision, his political power, and his will, Kemal had shaped a brand-new world from the ashes of the Ottoman Empire.

A NEW ECONOMIC POLICY

In October 1929, the Great Depression struck, setting off an international set of economic crises. Turkey suffered, as foreign demand for its agricultural exports declined. While the economies of the West—based on capitalist principles—struggled, the state-supported industries of Russia seemed to be thriving. It is not surprising, then, that Turkey decided to experiment with some government-sponsored industries and businesses. Kemal determined that the government would not interfere in agriculture but would test a five-year plan (another first for the Middle East) in which the state would develop certain industries, such as textiles, paper, glass, iron, steel, and chemicals. Although much-needed funding (from both Turkish and foreign governments) guaranteed the development of certain important businesses, the experiment was largely unsuccessful, in part because Turkey's greatest resource—its agriculture—was excluded from the experiment and in fact suffered as workers drifted from farms to cities in search of better-paying work.

The year 1933 marked a 10-year anniversary for the Turkish Republic and Kemal was re-elected for a third presidential term. Still, as Turkey pressed ahead on the path carved out by its leader, the world was changing. Adolph Hitler had risen to power in Germany, and the global community struggled to maintain peace through the efforts of the League of Nations. Meanwhile, Kemal introduced more reforms.

A new legal, weekly holiday from 1:00 P.M. on Saturday to Monday morning was established in 1935. The concept of a holy day of rest was not a Muslim custom, as it is in Christianity and Judaism. Moreover, the traditional Muslim day devoted to worship is Friday, not Sunday, which is a day not for rest but rather for bustling trade, particularly in the markets located around the mosque, and for public prayer. But the new law changed the day of rest to Sunday, bringing Turkey into line with other Western countries.

That same year brought an even greater change for the people. By January 1, 1935, all Turkish citizens were legally required to take last names. Prior to this date, the Turks, like many Muslims, did not use surnames. Children would be given a first name by which they would be known, plus their father's first name to indicate their family. Military cadets were generally identified by their first name and their place of birth. People of status often had honorary titles added to their names. But the new law changed all that. While military titles were kept, all other honorary or royal titles were eliminated.

This decision resulted in some short-term chaos, as citizens each chose a last name, some reflecting a special place or name that had significance for them. Soldiers frequently chose as their last name a place where an important battle had been fought. Others chose names that reflected their trade or business. Some chose adjectives that appealed to them, and names like Rock, Steel, and Iron were particularly popular. It was not unusual for members of the same family to choose different last names.

Kemal himself thought long and hard about the name he should take, a name befitting the leader of the Republic. At last, he settled on *Atatürk*, which means Father Turk, reflecting his view of himself as the Father of all Turks. From that point on, he would be known as Kemal Atatürk.

THE STORM CLOUDS OF WAR

While Turkish society was being reshaped in radical ways, the signs of international trouble were sweeping across Europe. The first disturbing event was the Italian invasion of Ethiopia in October 1935, in response to which Turkey supported the League of Nations' sanctions against Italy, motivated at least in part by the evidence that Italy was moving troops into the Dodecanese Islands off the Turkish coast. (Under the terms of the Treaty of Lausanne of 1923, Italy ruled the Dodecanese Islands; they are now part of Greece.) Then, in March 1936, Hitler reoccupied the Rhineland. Following a meeting with the nations that had signed the Treaty of Lausanne (apart, of course, from Italy), Turkey was granted the right to reintroduce troops into the straits and police the waterways to ensure that commercial ships could pass through safely. As the world braced for war, Turkey was aligning itself with Great Britain, its old enemy.

As the international scene grew more troubled, Atatürk's health grew poor. He had been a frequent and heavy drinker and, as he reached the age of 53, his habits of spending long days at work and long nights partying caught up with him. He began to suffer from cirrhosis of the liver caused by excessive drinking. His doctors ordered him to spend several months resting, but he resisted their advice. On May 19, 1938, he celebrated the nineteenth anniversary of his arrival at Samsun to launch the War of Independence with a parade through the capital, followed by a train trip south, where Turkey was gathering troops. The trip exhausted him, and would prove to be his last significant public appearance.

Experiencing liver failure and great discomfort, he agreed at last to his doctors' orders and moved to the yacht that had been presented to him by the Turkish people. He was kept informed of political affairs and government activities as the yacht lay anchored near Istanbul, but for the most part he rested and tried to recover from his draining illness. He would not succeed.

On October 16, 1938, Atatürk slipped into a coma. His family gathered around his bed, and political friends rushed from Ankara to Istanbul. He had given instructions as to the procedures to be followed after his death—specifically, there would be neither special religious services in mosques nor mass gatherings. The constitution would prevail, the government would continue, and a new president would be chosen by the Assembly.

But just as the instructions seemed to indicate that death was imminent, Atatürk emerged from his coma. The Assembly members returned to Ankara, and plans were made for Atatürk's appearance at the Republic Day celebration on October 29. But again, he fell ill, and could only listen from his bed to the bands marching on the shore past his yacht and the noise of the fireworks.

On November 8, Atatürk spoke his last words before slipping into a final coma. To his doctor he said, "Peace to you," which

In accordance with his wishes, no religious ceremonies or gatherings were organized after Mustafa Kemal Atatürk passed away. Admired by his people and respected for his modern reforms, Atatürk laid in state for seven days before being buried. Fifteen years later, he was moved to the Turkish capital, Ankara, in an official procession attended by 200,000 Turkish citizens *(above)*.

is the traditional Muslim reply to a greeting. Two days later, he died.

For seven days, mourners filed past their leader's body as it lay in state at Dolmabahce Palace. Just as he had dictated, the republic and the government continued. A new president was elected—Ismet Inönü, who had served as prime minister for many years before falling briefly out of favor with the president. He was the only candidate, and he was elected unanimously.

The mourning for Atatürk was real and heartfelt. For the people of Turkey, his death represented an end to an era of extraordinary transformation. He had given them first a sense of national pride through his victories over the Greeks, the West, and the sultan, and then a nation worthy of that pride. He had empowered them to become the masters of their own fate, no longer ruled by a monarch but instead governed by representatives they chose themselves. He had given them a changed language and a new identity. Unlike many revolutionaries that would follow him in the Middle East, he resisted the temptation to create a military dictatorship based on violence and repression. Instead, he built a system of government designed to outlast one man. He built a society whose values were based on economic progress, rather than military victory.

Without Atatürk, a modern Turkey might never have existed. And now, his people would have to discover whether a modern Turkey could exist without him.

5

Turkey After Atatürk

The republic Atatürk had shaped was strong, designed to outlast a single man's life. He had put a system in place to ensure an orderly transfer of leadership, and the newly elected president was an experienced official. Inönü shared his predecessor's belief in the need for Turkey to develop into a modern country, rooted in strong government rather than confining religious beliefs. Many of the policies that had begun under Atatürk were continued after his death. The effort to expand educational opportunities beyond the cities and into the countryside was aided by the creation of "village institutes," where rural farmers and peasants were trained to serve as schoolteachers. State ballet and opera companies were formed to ensure that the Turkish people could create and enjoy the finest Western culture.

As fascist regimes in Germany, Italy, and Japan denounced the evils of modern society, seeking to pull their countries back to an earlier, idealized past, Inönü continued to lead Turkey forward. With the world splitting into two sides in preparation for another war, the Turkish people were fortunate to have the diplomatically skillful Inönü as their leader. His experience, derived from years of serving as Atatürk's prime minister, guaranteed him a certain measure of respect from the world leaders with whom he met. He negotiated alliances with France and Great Britain and simultaneously signed a non-aggression treaty with Germany. These were astute moves, but they also made Turkey a haven for spies of both sides during World War II. Popular support in Turkey lay with the Allies, but most politicians believed at the war's beginning that the Axis countries would win,

Village institutes *(above)* were strongly supported by Prime Minister Ismet Inönü and were the backbone of education in rural areas. Designed to train local farmers and peasants to become teachers in isolated regions of the country, the program successfully increased the number of primary schools in Turkey.

particularly when, in 1941, German victories in the Balkans brought the German army to within 100 miles of Istanbul.

It was only toward the end of the war, when an Allied victory seemed certain, that Turkey abandoned its policy of neutrality and came out on the side of the Allies. In this way, Turkey was able to avoid the devastating kind of war that had crippled its economy and ripped its land apart at the beginning of the twentieth century. It also permitted the republic to join the United Nations at its founding.

Many Turkish businessmen profited during the war due to the opportunities for foreign trade. Turkey had no formal system of taxation, and as the government struggled to meet its expenses, a decision was made to collect revenue through an emergency tax. This went into effect on November 12, 1942, and created almost immediate chaos.

Those who benefited the most from the wartime economy were the farmers, who were mainly Muslim Turks, and the Istanbul business community, consisting mainly of Greeks, Jews, and Armenians. It quickly became clear that the tax was completely biased, both in amount and in enforcement. Businesses were to be taxed at a rate of 50 percent to 75 percent. Large farm owners, however, would be required to pay no more than 5 percent. For the vast majority of taxpayers, it was left to local tax boards to determine how much each individual should pay, without gathering any basic information, such as how much that person earned or had saved. The decisions of these boards were all final, and payment was due within 15 days. Taxpayers were classified based on their religion and nationality, with non-Muslims paying much more than Muslim citizens. After a month, the names of those who had failed to pay their taxes, as well as the amounts they owed, were published, and shortly thereafter they were deported to labor camps. The vast majority of those arrested and sent to the labor camps were Greeks, Jews, and Armenians. It was a sad moment for the republic.

This tax policy enjoyed strong support from the same sources that had stood firmly behind Germany in the war, and it was not until Allied victory seemed certain, and Allied leadership criticized this clear example of intolerance, that the punished were gradually brought back from the labor camps. Foreign citizens were unjustly taxed and clearly suffered discrimination; only foreign pressure corrected this appalling situation.

THE POST-WAR WORLD

After the war had ended, Turkey enjoyed new and stronger relationships with the United States and Great Britain. Both countries were concerned about the Russian leader Stalin and his plans to expand Communist control over Eastern Europe and to station troops in the straits to ensure their passage into the Aegean and Mediterranean seas. They needed Turkey as a buffer, a country that would resist the Soviet influence.

Links with the democratic governments in Washington and London sparked public interest in moving away from the single-party system that had marked Turkish government for many years. The Republican People's Party had shaped the country, but now the Turkish people were interested in expanding the types of political representation available to them. In addition, Turkey's participation in the newly formed United Nations was exposing it to discussions on the importance of democratically elected governments and the need for more than one party to ensure fair and representative government.

A group of disenchanted Republican People's Party members, especially merchants and farmers who disliked the state economic controls their party favored and desired greater change than their party and its leaders offered, decided to form a new party, one they called the Democratic Party. Many of their fellow politicians viewed them as traitors, and at first it seemed quite possible that their efforts would be stamped out, perhaps by force. But Inönü, showing wisdom and restraint, instead recommended that, to avoid becoming a dictatorship,

Turkey should permit the formation of an opposition party. Only two types of political parties were banned: Communist and religious.

The postwar Turkey was marked by the movement of greater numbers of citizens into urban areas. More citizens were becoming educated. They read the newspaper and kept informed about political developments. Overall communication increased as more households had telephones and radios. It was a time

As postwar Turkey formed political relationships with Western powers, they also further developed their education, communication, and transportation systems within the country. Pictured, new roads linking major Turkish cities encouraged travel and commerce within the country.

of greater mobility as the public system of roads and railways expanded and improved. Some Turks were taking jobs in Europe, a trend that grew during the next two decades and continues to have a profound impact. The Turkey Atatürk had dreamed of—a literate, educated, cultured, and well-traveled society—was becoming a reality.

On May 14, 1950, Turkey held its first free and open elections. The Democrats, appealing to a desire for change and with firm support from certain groups that were distinctly opposed to the People's Party (such as religious leaders, wealthy landowners, and a newly created middle class), won a majority of the seats in the Assembly, and Inönü was obliged to resign. It is yet another tribute to the strong government set in place in Turkey that, after 27 years in power, the leadership was able to change hands peacefully.

Although the party Atatürk had founded would never again win a majority of seats in the Assembly, his memory was far from dimmed following the election. The new president, Celal Bayar, a banker, had served as prime minister under Atatürk from 1937 to 1939, and one of his first acts as president was to place the picture of the Father of Turks on Turkish stamps and money. But the new government was less firm in its restrictions on the role of Islam. The principles of democracy from which the ruling party had taken its inspiration required freedom of expression, and gradually religious leaders, who had kept silent and been restrained from asserting power during the years of Atatürk, were able once again to advocate publicly a return to Islamic values and traditions. Mosques were rebuilt throughout Turkey, and Bayar's government allowed the faithful to be called to worship in the traditional Arabic rather than in Turkish.

Religious education was restored in the public schools starting in early 1949, when parents were permitted to enroll their children in religious classes for two hours on Saturday afternoon. Many did. Little more than a year later, religious education became mandatory in the fourth and fifth grades. Where a short time before, the Islamic classes were offered only if parents specifically requested them for their children, now parents were forced to make a specific request that their children *not* be enrolled in the classes.

For four years, the Democratic Party succeeded in its policies, and Turkey enjoyed a period of economic prosperity. The Democrats' plans for growth relied less on government intervention in industry and more on agriculture. The government boosted the resources available to farmers by expanding the amount of land under cultivation and importing more tractors to increase production on that land. In the beginning, these efforts worked well. But as the economy slowed, and public dissatisfaction with the new policies increased, the Democratic Party became less "democratic" in its system of government. Fearing challenges from other parties, the Democrats took over the newspaper of the Republican People's Party and seized its property. By February 1954, the Democrats had passed a new censorship law, stating that anyone who published "inaccurate" information about the government (in other words, anything that was thought to be harmful to Turkey politically or economically) would be imprisoned.

There were some within the Democratic Party who objected to these heavy-handed tactics, and many of them left to form their own separate but short-lived party, known as the Freedom Party. Elections in 1958 gave the Democrats a victory, but many questioned the results, believing the votes had been incorrectly reported or somehow rigged. Matters came to a head in February 1960. The Republican People's Party had organized a meeting where the former president Inönü was scheduled to speak. The police were sent in to break up the meeting, angering opposition party members. Two months later, the Democratic Party in the Assembly created a commission whose duties would be to investigate members of the Republican People's Party and other opposition groups. The commission would be allowed to search property and people and to arrest anyone deemed to be a threat to the state.

These actions outraged Turkish citizens. Students formed protest groups in Istanbul and Ankara. The government retaliated by declaring martial law in both cities. Such use of the military to quiet rebellion in the streets of Turkey's two largest cities would prove to be a costly mistake for the leadership. The army quickly decided that the Democrats had gone too far. Early in the morning of May 27, 1960, General Cemal Gürsel led a team to arrest the politically powerful Democratic prime minister Adnan Menderes and the members of his cabinet. The military had overthrown the government.

THE MILITARY RULES

As their first act, General Gürsel and 37 of the officers who had led the takeover announced that they would form the National Unity Committee, assuming for themselves the powers that had previously belonged to the Assembly. In the new government, Gürsel declared that he would serve as prime minister (a position that had, in recent years, become more powerful than the presidency), as well as the head of state and minister of defense. The leaders of the Democratic Party were charged with various crimes, including corruption and violating the constitution. Following a quick trial, Menderes and two other officials were executed, and other party members were imprisoned or put under house arrest.

While the National Unity Committee had no immediate interest in sharing power, it did take steps to eliminate, for the future, a concentration of power in a single political party. A new constitution was drafted stating that Turkey would now have a Senate as well as its Assembly (the House of Representatives), and establishing a new Supreme or Constitutional Court chosen by the executive and charged with approving laws passed by the Senate and Assembly. The new constitution also granted the

Army tanks try to disperse a crowd of Islamic protestors in February 1997 in the small town of Sincan, outside the Turkish capital, Ankara. The army's presence served as a warning against religious activities in this country where the military considers itself the guarantor of the secular system and has toppled governments several times in Turkey's recent past.

right to form unions, as well as mandating a system for universal medical care and social security.

After setting up systems to protect the rights of opposition parties, the military decided to step down in favor of a civilian government. General elections were held in 1961, but no single party won a majority of the seats. General Gürsel was elected president. A coalition formed between the Republican People's Party and the newly formed Justice Party brought Inönü back as a political player, but only briefly. By 1965, the young Justice Party had gained in strength and numbers and won a majority of the votes, electing its young leader Süleyman Demirel to the position of prime minister.

The military believed so strongly in the ideals of Atatürk and saw itself as guardian of his policies and heritage (a belief that continues to this day) that its interventions in government continued for the next several decades. Each time it saw the country straying from what it considered the core beliefs of the constitution, or being overly influenced by politicians who placed their own needs over those of their country, the military stepped in. In March 1971, it forced a change in government. In September 1980, it seized control of the country when militant Marxists and Muslims were openly fighting against each other. In June 1998, it again intervened in response to a rise in fundamentalism that seemed to signal a shift away from the ideals of Atatürk. Despite all these efforts, the stability the country had enjoyed under Atatürk would never again be completely replicated.

MORE PARTIES, MORE CONFUSION

The policies that the military had installed to prevent a single group from seizing power engendered a multitude of smaller parties appealing to more specialized interests. The development of trade unions, coupled with increasing numbers of people moving to cities or living and working in Europe before returning to Turkey, encouraged more left-leaning political groups to form, including the Confederation of Reformist Workers' Unions (whose supporters were mostly trade union members), Dev Cenç (a youth movement calling for revolution), the Workers' Party of Turkey (a socialist group), and even the People's Liberation Army of Turkey (an armed guerrilla movement). Meanwhile, the Democrats were released from prison, and by 1969 they were once more allowed to form a new Democratic Party and solicit members. On the right, groups that had split off from the Republican People's Party included the National Action Party and the National Order Party (both groups calling for a return to Islamic values and a renewed focus on Turkish nationalism).

While this wide array of choices for voters meant that many different groups had a voice in politics, it also meant that it was nearly impossible for any single group to muster enough political support to accomplish significant initiatives without being a part of a coalition in both houses of parliament. Many of these parties were armed and favored violent means to settle their differences. Uprisings in Kurdistan increased the perception that the government had lost control. On March 12, 1971, the commanders of the three military branches announced that they would step in to ensure the formation of a strong and credible government intended to follow in the tradition of Atatürk by imposing reforms that followed the spirit of the constitution. Demirel was forced to resign. For the next 30 months, Turkey would be run by a series of governments that essentially were installed and directed by the military. Their main task was to restore law and order and in 11 of Turkey's 67 provinces, martial law was declared to accomplish this. They arrested anyone suspected of revolutionary activities against the government (including those guilty only of speaking out against the military takeover). While the military-supported governments proclaimed its principles of freedom and democracy, its actions showed quite another side.

By the spring of 1973, the military officers had reached a difficult crossroad. Their support within the weakened government was dwindling. They had two choices: (1) to take over the government completely, removing any non-military people from power, or (2) to allow free elections to be held. They chose the second option, and the elections were held in October 1973. The army's candidate for the presidency was defeated and, for the next seven years, political power shifted wildly among a series of small parties and weak governments. Political violence escalated as extremist groups tried to seize power through aggressive tactics. As the governments changed hands swiftly, averaging a new one every two years, corruption rose and public confidence in all politicians sank.

For a third time, the military stepped in. Early in the morning of September 12, 1980, General Kenan Evren overthrew the government, arrested the leaders of all major parties, and set up himself and five officers as the National Security Council, intended to be a temporary military government. They dissolved the parliament, all political parties, and even the unions, and put martial law into effect throughout Turkey. The public largely supported these actions to restore order and bring an end to the chaos.

One of the principal goals of the military regime was to eliminate the violence that had become a hallmark of the political process. Terrorists were hunted down and arrested. Concern about the spread of a particularly violent and revolutionary form of Islam (inspired by the Islamic revolution that overthrew the government in nearby Iran) spurred the government to crack down on all extremists. Guerrilla warfare was becoming a serious problem among the Kurdish population.

The military was determined to correct, officially, some of the mistakes of the past. In 1982, a new constitution that changed the system of government in Turkey was drafted and approved. This new constitution created a president with greater powers than in the past. Elected for a seven-year term, the president was empowered to appoint the prime minister and dismiss the parliament. The parliament was reduced from two groups (the Assembly and the Senate) to a single representative body. The constitution also eliminated the influence of smaller bodies by stating that a party had to receive at least 10 percent of the votes to win a seat in the parliament.

The new constitution called for elections in 1983. The military had hoped the parties it supported would win handily, but instead it was the Motherland Party, a coalition of liberal, nationalist, and Islamic groups appealing to those disenchanted with the military's strong-arm tactics, that won a majority of seats in the parliament. More important for Turks discouraged by inflation and economic troubles, the Motherland Party was led by the well-known economist Turgut Özal.

Özal's prescription for economic healing included less dependence on government controls and an increase in foreign trade. During the Motherland Party's rule of Turkey from 1983 to 1987, these policies were quite successful. Neighboring Iran and Iraq were at war, and oil prices fell. The opportunities for trade were strong, and Turkey's economy grew rapidly. But the period of prosperity did not last. A recession crippled world economies in the late 1980s, and Turkey felt its effects as well. Unemployment and inflation hit the country hard.

As Özal's government struggled to deal with economic troubles, it found itself facing an even more serious problem in the southeastern provinces. Violent outbursts from the dissatisfied Kurds had grown in intensity and frequency. Now Turks were fighting a war—a war for independence—within their own borders.

The Kurds

T he Kurdish population has for many years sparked fierce debate, both within and beyond the borders of Turkey, about exactly what constitutes a nation and what qualifies a people to govern its own territory. The Kurds, more than any other people, were left behind in the scattered ashes of the Ottoman Empire. Living principally in the region where Turkey, Iran, Syria, and Iraq come together, they are divided artificially by borders and territorial claims into four separate countries, when in reality they are a single people unified by customs and language. For many years they had sought independence from the nations that governed them, yet no nation was willing to grant them self-rule.

In Turkey's view, the Kurdish region was economically valuable and not something simply to be handed away. As an agricultural center, it was important principally for its production of cotton and tobacco. It also contained valuable oil and water resources. Nonetheless, the region was wracked by poverty. The great gains Atatürk and his successors had achieved in modernizing Turkey provided little benefit to the Kurds.

To understand why the Turkish government so strongly resisted the Kurds' calls for independence, it is important to

(opposite) The Kurds have inhabited parts of present-day Turkey, Iran, Syria, and Iraq since the 2400s B.C, in a region often referred to as Kurdistan. Kurdish communities can also be found in Lebanon, Armenia, and Azerbaijan, as well as some European countries and the United States.

The Kurds

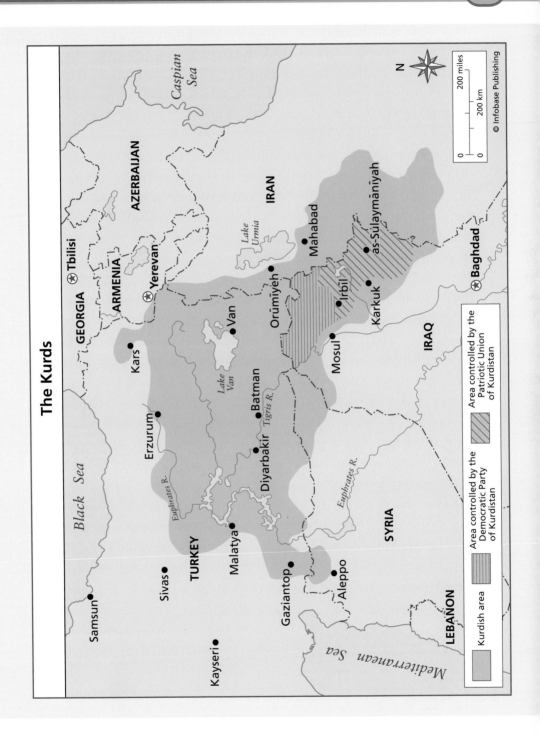

remember how bitterly the wars for independence were fought to ensure that no more of Turkish territory slipped away after the breakup of the Ottoman Empire. All successors have held fast to this principle—that the boundaries of Turkey were defined in 1919, and no part of it should be given up without a fight.

The Kurdish calls for independence were certainly not a new development but dated back almost to the founding of modern Turkey and are reflected in the 1920 Treaty of Sèvres. Atatürk's early reform policies were deeply divisive in the Kurdish region. Since the Kurds wanted a Muslim state, the decision to abolish the caliphate was alarming to them. More disturbing still were Mustafa Kemal's later steps to strengthen Turkey's national identity, but which had the effect of diminishing the Kurdish character of the southeastern region. Places were no longer known by their Kurdish names, but only by Turkish ones. Turks moved into the Kurdish region to fill the middle- and senior-level government positions. The Kurdish language could no longer be spoken in courts or used in schools, a law that drastically affected the quality of education and legal representation available to the Kurdish people.

The result was inevitable: a revolt among the Kurds in 1925 as the effects of these Turkification policies became clear. Martial law was declared in all of Kurdistan, hundreds of rebels and suspected rebels were executed, and other brutal actions were yet to come. Many Kurds were forcibly evacuated to western Anatolia. Villages were burnt, and their inhabitants— men, women, and children—were killed. Cattle and other animals were seized and removed, effectively condemning the people to starvation. All religious organizations were shut down. In Turkey, Kurds were officially referred to as "mountain Turks."

Such cruel policing of this segment of the population became a routine assignment for the Turkish army. In fact, the majority of Turkish military activities in the past 50 years, with few exceptions, have been against the Kurds, not against aggressive invaders or foreign armies.

The rebellions continued to break out as the Kurds fought fiercely, both in Turkey and in neighboring regions, for the survival of their culture and people. In June 1934, Turkey passed a strict law intended to stamp out the Kurdish rebellion for good. The law essentially divided Turkey into three parts: (1) regions reserved for people who already possessed the necessary "Turkish culture"; (2) regions where people of "non-Turkish culture" were to be moved in order to be educated in Turkish language and culture; and (3) regions that were to be evacuated. It is clear that the goal of this law was to eliminate significant Kurdish populations from any region, but the very real problems of relocating the 3 million Kurdish people in small groups throughout the rest of Turkey prevented this law from being fully carried out.

The Republican People's Party, first under Atatürk and later his successors, carried out an effective campaign to quiet rebellions—whether from Kurdistan in the southeast or other parts of Turkey. But the opening up of political power to other parties revived the cries for independence that had been silenced for many years. As the Democratic Party won power and restored a religious presence to the state, mosques and places of worship once more began to issue the call for a return to the traditional Islamic values that had flourished under the Ottomans.

The Kurds first rallied behind the Democrats, but soon became disillusioned when the reality of their policies differed greatly from what had been promised. Political freedom, however, sparked a revival of Kurdish separatism, and the Kurdish homeland became an important campaign site for the many different political parties that swept across Turkey, including a secret (because it was illegal) Kurdish party. The region was poor; increased mechanization and modern but costlier farming methods had left many farmers unemployed. The people were under-educated and living closely together. More significant, although

Turkey's population was holding fairly steady, the population in Kurdistan was nearly doubling.

THE PKK (THE KURDISTAN WORKERS' PARTY)

These were the conditions that concerned Özal (who himself was part Kurdish) and his government in the 1980s, when news of increasing numbers of rebellions in Kurdish territory reached Ankara. In the early 1980s, the violence was so widespread that two-thirds of the Turkish army was patrolling the Kurdish region to keep the peace there and, possibly, to intimidate the

Oppression of the Kurds led to the formation of the Kurdistan Workers Party, known as the PKK. Intent on defending Kurdish and workers' rights, this organization initiated rebel attacks against the public, and also targeted tourist sites in Turkey. *Above*, bomb experts search for evidence after a Kurdish rebel threw herself in front of a bus with a bomb strapped to her waist.

Kurds. At first, it seemed that the violence was being contained. But then, in August 1984, a new series of attacks began against Turkish forces. The source was the Kurdistan Workers' Party (PKK).

This group was unusual among Turkish political parties because its members were drawn largely from the working class. The PKK fought not merely for Kurdish rights, but also for workers' rights. It was rebelling against the horrible living conditions of the average Turk while wealthy merchants and the ruling elite enjoyed prosperity and the benefits of wealth in far-distant Ankara and Istanbul. The PKK was intent on launching not merely a civil war, but also a class war. And its targets were not only soldiers: In addition to attacking military bases and ambushing troops, the PKK also began killing wealthy landowners and seizing their estates.

The government drastically increased the number of soldiers sent to patrol Kurdistan. By 1987, a state of emergency was declared in eight Kurdish provinces and a governor-general was appointed to coordinate the efforts of the various forces fighting the PKK. The governor-general was given wide-ranging powers, including the authority to evacuate villages if he felt it was necessary. Torture was common, and hundreds of villagers were routinely arrested and beaten until they confessed to aiding the PKK efforts.

These efforts backfired horribly. Initially, a minority of Kurdish villagers had supported the PKK's campaign of intimidation and its arbitrary murders of landlords and village guards. But as the government's violent and brutal tactics eclipsed those used by the PKK and resulted in Kurdish families living in constant fear of imprisonment and abuse, the number of Kurds supporting the PKK increased steadily.

Hoping to weaken the PKK and gain popular Turkish support, President Özal announced that any Turkish publishing house that "falsely reflected events in the region" would be closed down. The same law gave the governor-general of Kurdistan the right to relocate anyone he chose to an area determined by the government. Hundreds of villages were burned following the passing of this law, leaving thousands of people homeless.

Turks as well as Kurds began to protest against these actions. The images of their own citizens turned into refugees by the Turkish military offended the average Turks, and the government soon realized that the crisis had been transformed from a regional to a national one.

By 1992, President Özal drastically changed his policy toward the Kurdish situation and called for recognition of the PKK as a possible participant in Turkey's political system. The PKK responded with a brief cease-fire in March of 1993, but the overtures for peaceful compromise made by Özal vanished at his death on April 17, 1993. The new president, Süleyman Demirel, was less willing to negotiate with the PKK, and ordered the army to capitalize on the cease-fire by rounding up as many PKK fighters as it could find. In six weeks, the army killed about 100 people (fighters and civilians), arrested hundreds more, and resumed its destruction of homes and whole villages. The chance for peace had vanished.

A WIDENING CONFLICT

President Demirel had appointed Tansu Ciller as Turkey's first female prime minister, but she was unable or unwilling to challenge the military officers. The violence and intensity of the struggle grew at a frightening pace. Towns were subjected to military assaults. Civilians died in numbers equal to the soldiers and guerrilla fighters. The recently formed Kurdish political party, the People's Labour Party (HEP), was banned in July 1993.

The PKK responded by bringing the conflict to other parts of Turkey. Tourist sites in southern Turkey were attacked. European tourists in Kurdish areas were seized as hostages. Kurdish separatists attacked Turkish embassies and business locations in Europe. By the end of 1993, it was reported that 10,000 people had died since the conflicts first began in 1984. Within one year, that number would double.

The national nightmare was rapidly becoming a foreign policy disaster. As Turkey sought to establish itself as an active and democratic participant in the international community, these human rights abuses against its own people made foreign investors wary. And as more Kurds were heard calling for autonomy, or the right to govern their own region, rather than for complete independence and separation from Turkey, the horrific

Protestors from Great Britain's Turkish community marched through London to call for Great Britain to be more active in opposing the PKK. The PKK has frequently used violence and intimidation in its campaign for Kurdish rights.

response of the Turkish government was increasingly difficult to understand or excuse.

The dreams of Atatürk for Turkey—a strong nation unified by language, education, and Westernized ideas—seemed noble on the surface, but they have left an expensive legacy. The 12 million Kurds living in Turkey continue to pay the price.

Modern Turkey

For much of the early part of the twentieth century, Turkey upheld its Westernization program in conducting its foreign policy. Turkey joined the North Atlantic Treaty Organization (NATO) in 1952, and applied to join the European Economic Community (EEC) in 1959, to which it belongs in a limited way. It has, for many years, sought membership in the European Union (EU), but this has been the subject of great debate, both within the EU (from critics of Turkey's actions against the Kurds and those who fear a massive influx of Turkish immigrants) and within Turkey itself (from Muslim militants who preach the need to turn away from the West).

Many of the difficulties Turkey currently faces in matters of foreign policy stem from the actions it has taken against Cyprus. Located in the eastern Mediterranean, some 40 miles south of Turkey, Cyprus is the third largest island in that sea, after Sicily and Sardinia. It was one of the few territories from the Ottoman Empire that remained a British colony; 80 percent of its inhabitants were and are Greek-speaking Christians. By the 1950s, the people of Cyprus were demanding what they felt was their long-overdue independence.

What should have been a simple, straightforward process—to grant independence or not—turned out to be anything but. Not only Great Britain, but also Greece and Turkey felt they had a specific and strategic interest in Cyprus. The majority of the population of Cyprus speaks Greek, and traces of Greeks on Cyprus date back to its earliest recorded history. A frequent target of invaders because of its strategic position, Cyprus was conquered by Ottoman Turks in the 1500s, and it remained a part of the

Ottoman Empire until 1878, when the island was leased to the British in exchange for British support against the Russian army. When the Ottoman Empire sided with Germany in World War I, the British formally annexed Cyprus and in 1925 proclaimed it a British colony.

The Turks, Greeks, and British all managed to live in relatively peaceful coexistence until Cyprian demands for independence became more frequent and were, each time, denied by the British. Greece supported a plan to unify Cyprus with Greece. Turkey objected, arguing that the island's proximity to Turkey posed a strategic threat. The Turkish position was that Cyprus should either remain British or be divided into separate Turkish and Greek regions.

The debate caused tension within NATO and the United Nations, as the international community was faced with the uneasy prospect of choosing sides between two members of those organizations. Ultimately, following a series of diplomatic negotiations, it was announced on August 16, 1960, that Cyprus would become an independent state, although independence was relative. Great Britain was allowed to maintain two military bases in the southern and eastern regions of the island and Greece and Turkey were also allowed to maintain small military units and to police their respective communities. The system of government was similarly restricted. The president would always be Greek; the vice president, Turkish. Each community would be judged by its own separate courts; legal cases involving both communities would be decided in trials presided over by two judges.

This awkward arrangement served only to further divide the people living on Cyprus. Tensions rose steadily until July 1974 when the Greek president was overthrown in a coup and a new Greek government installed. Its leaders proclaimed that Cyprus must be united with Greece. Turkey responded quickly and with force. Early in the morning of July 20, Turkish forces began landing on the northern part of Cyprus, both by sea and from the air, as landing craft pulled up on the shores and paratroopers dropped into the Turkish communities. For several days, the Turkish troops pushed steadily inward until they occupied nearly 40 percent of the island, sending thousands of Greek refugees into the remaining portions of Cyprus.

The prospect of Turkey and Greece going to war became increasingly real as the dispute widened to include arguments over territory in the Aegean Sea. Initial NATO response was tentative, designed to limit the crisis rather than end it decisively. (Both Greece and Turkey were NATO members.) In the fall of 1974, the United States took the unexpected step of declaring an arms embargo against Turkey, freezing the delivery of $200 million in weapons. The embargo lasted for several years, until U.S. president Jimmy Carter took decisive steps to end it. But the effects of the Cyprus situation, and the various countries' roles in it, are felt to this day.

For Turkey, the experience in Cyprus proved that a purely pro-Western diplomatic policy would be inadequate to its interests. Turkey felt betrayed by the response of its Western allies, particularly the United States, to the initially aggressive action of the Greeks, and angered at the arms embargo resulting from what it claimed was merely an action taken to protect the Turkish community on Cyprus. Turkey reached out to the Soviet Union, forming trade alliances with a power it had once regarded as its greatest enemy. When the Soviet Union collapsed in 1989, the Turkish government formed agreements with many of its former republics, including those in the Balkans and Central Asia.

While Greece has been admitted to the European Union, Turkey's repeated attempts to gain entry to this important organization have yet to succeed. For Turkey, the economic importance of Europe is clear—about 50 percent of Turkey's exports are destined for Europe and, in return, approximately 50 percent of its imports come from there. Many Turks travel to Europe to get higher-paying jobs than they can find at home. To the Turks, it is particularly disturbing that Cyprus became a member of the EU in 2004, while Turkey is still considered a "candidate for membership" with no fixed date set for its inclusion.

Turkish links with NATO have continued, despite frequent disagreements over strategic and diplomatic issues. In Bosnia, Turkey sided with Muslims against the Serbs and actively participated in UN and NATO actions in the region. Similarly, Turkey supported UN actions against Iraq in the Persian Gulf War in 1990, allowing UN and NATO troops access to its military bases. The decision proved an expensive one, as the subsequent UN embargo against Iraq would cost Turkey millions of dollars when revenue from oil pipelines passing through Turkey disappeared.

THE ROLE OF ISLAM

As dissatisfaction with government policies spreads among the people, the conditions are ripe for revolt, and the threat of Islamic militant action is a constant concern. The government continues to waver between opening the door slightly to increase religious freedom and stamping out all Islamic activities and particularly political parties lest they become too powerful and steer Turkey backward in time to the days of the caliph. One issue that currently dominates political debate is whether to revoke the ban on women wearing the Islamic head scarf in schools and government buildings.

The fear of an Islamic revival has dictated much of recent Turkish policy toward the activities of political parties. Since 1980, there has been a marked increase in visible displays of Islamic culture in Turkey—more Islamic books and prayer manuals are being published, more women are wearing head scarves, more mosques are being built, and religious classes are becoming increasingly popular.

In elections in December 1995, the political party that won the largest portion of the vote was the Islamic Welfare Party. A shift in thinking was occurring, as support for the traditional ideals and values represented by the Welfare Party came not only from rural areas but also from the cities. The Welfare Party urged stronger alliances with Middle Eastern nations and less reliance

Balancing the religious and secular viewpoints of the people has been a constant struggle for the Turkish government. Following the example of their first president, Mustafa Kemal Atatürk, officials have decreased the presence of religion in schools and have banned headscarves from universities and government offices. Still, there has been an increase in public displays of Islamic culture in Turkey.

on Europe and the United States. It encouraged an increased role for Islam in public life. It failed to form a successful coalition with other groups, but its ability to garner support signaled an important shift in political thought and led to government crackdowns on several Islamic political parties.

One of the most infamous attempts at suppression is what is known in Turkey as "the process of 28 February," referring to a campaign begun in February 1999, spearheaded by military officers who see themselves as the guardians of Turkish secularism, to eradicate political Islam from education, business, and other activities. Businesses suspected of financing Islamic political parties were penalized, and professors accused of encouraging Islamic thought (known as "reactionary views") in the universities were barred from serving as deans or from holding other high administrative positions.

One of the most prominent victims of this 1999 campaign was the mayor of Istanbul, Recep Erdoğan. At the time a member of the Welfare Party, Erdoğan was deposed as mayor, arrested, and sentenced to 10 months in prison (he was released after 4) following a rally at which he recited a poem. The poem had been written by a nationalist poet at a time when Turkey was threatened by foreign armies, and included the line: "The mosques are our barracks, their minarets our bayonets, their domes our shields." Because he recited this at the rally, Erdoğan was found guilty of encouraging "divisive religious passions."

The Welfare Party later evolved into the pro-Islamist Virtue Party, which was also banned in 2001. Gradually, the members of the Welfare and Virtue parties reformed into a less strident, more reform-minded party, the Justice and Development (AK) Party in 2002.

The leader of the AK Party was Recep Erdoğan. In the 2002 elections, the AK Party won a majority of the seats in Turkey's parliament, and, in February 2003, Erdoğan became Turkey's prime minister.

Prime Minister Erdoğan has worked hard to achieve membership for Turkey in the European Union. As part of this effort, his government has strived to comply with an economic program set up by the International Monetary Fund to solve Turkey's economic problems and has rewritten laws to meet European standards. One of his most controversial acts occurred in April 2007, when he announced his decision to nominate Abdullah Gül as Turkey's new president. As detailed in the first chapter of this book, following elections and several rounds of voting, the outcome was Turkey's first Islamist president.

FOREIGN POLICY

Turkey's geography continues to define it less than a hundred years after Atatürk took steps to ensure that Turkey would, in the future, be defined as European rather than Middle Eastern. Nowhere is this clearer than in the matter of foreign policy.

The Turkish government has worked over the years to develop ties with western countries to help improve their nation's standard of living. Former foreign minister Abdullah Gül *(now Turkey's president, right)* and Prime Minister Recep Erdoğan *(left)*, have openly negotiated terms with European officials on the recognition of Cyprus, a former Turkish territory.

Turkey's efforts to join the EU have continually been stalled, and in recent years the country has begun to look to other partners in the Middle East—particularly Iran, Saudi Arabia, and Syria—for trade. The decision to back the U.S. military campaign to drive Iraq out of Kuwait in 1990–1991 proved extremely costly for Turkey. By enforcing United Nations sanctions and cutting off the flow of Iraq's oil exports through Turkish pipelines, deploying Turkish troops along the border with Iraq, and allowing the United States to use Turkish bases for its aerial campaign, Turkey had hoped to cement economic ties with the United States.

But Turkey won few economic benefits for its efforts and indeed lost billions of dollars in pipeline fees and trade. At the same time, the war increased the conflict within Turkey, particularly among its Kurdish population. Following the Gulf War, a de facto Kurdish state was created in northern Iraq, a state that enjoyed a certain amount of Western protection. The PKK used those bases in northern Iraq to launch attacks against Turkish targets and add to the rise of Kurdish nationalism in Turkey. Turkey responded with air strikes and a land invasion into Kurdish territory in northern Iraq.

In recent years, Turkey has been far more reluctant to allow the United States to use Turkish air bases as a launching pad for military campaigns. In the U.S.-led invasion of Iraq in 2003, Turkey refused to allow the United States to station combat aircraft at its bases or use those bases to fly combat missions in the Middle East or Persian Gulf.

The U.S. invasion of Iraq in 2003 posed additional foreign policy problems for Turkey. The invasion deposed Iraq's leader, Saddam Hussein, and in the power vacuum that followed the invasion and overthrow of Hussein's regime, Iraq has become embroiled in guerrilla warfare and, some charge, international terrorism. Kurds within Iraq have been striving to establish their own state on the southern border of Turkey. Turkish officials fear that this could increase the separatist movement within Turkey's Kurdish population and inspire additional attacks.

Indeed, violence attributed to the PKK has increased in Turkey in recent years. Since January 2006, the PKK has launched repeated attacks on Turkey from northern Iraq, attacks that target both military and civilian targets. Prime Minister Erdoğan repeatedly called for U.S. military assistance to eliminate PKK training camps in northern Iraq; the United States' reluctance to take firm action against the Kurds in northern Iraq has caused an increase in anti-American sentiment in Turkey. Ultimately, in late 2007 Turkey began launching attacks across the border, against what it claimed were Kurdish bases in the Kandil Mountains in northern Iraq.

A DREAM UNFULFILLED

Turkey today remains a nation of contrasts. Its culture reflects both Arabic and Western influences. It struggles to shake off the dusty legacy of its Ottoman past and yet embraces the important role it plays within the Islamic world. It clings to the dreams of Western democratic ideals first outlined by Atatürk while it fiercely resists the demand of its Kurdish population to govern itself and eliminates political parties whose views and popularity seem to threaten the government. It supports the need for international partnerships, and yet turns away when its partners express concern about Turkey's human rights record.

Turkey is adjacent to so many potentially troublesome regions that its importance in global politics is clear. Its presence is a balance to the civil strife in Iraq and the more militant regimes in Iran. Its strict secular policy stands in marked contrast to the governments of most of its neighbors. In many ways, Turkey has become the important Western ally that Atatürk had planned. And yet its actions in recent years have made it clear that Turkish policy is dictated by national, rather than international, concerns.

Atatürk's dreams for the young nation have, in some ways, been realized. The Republic of Turkey, the country that rose from the ashes of the Ottoman Empire, has become a nation with

Above, two Turkish students walk by the main campus of Istanbul University. As Turkey continues to develop relationships with other countries and international organizations, the country itself is also renegotiating its views on religious tolerance. Although a pro-secular government is still preferred by many Turks, the growing acceptance of Muslim traditions is shaping the image of this modern Muslim country.

clear boundaries and a clear identity. Its people are Turks, most speak their own Turkish language, and they fiercely resist any attempt to redraw their borders or disperse their land.

And yet the very vision that freed Turkey from domination by European powers has still left it imprisoned. The effort to keep Turkey from returning to the days of rule by a caliph have left it uneasy with any strong expression of religion and uncertain about whether such a balance can be achieved when both the prime minister and president represent Islamic parties. The inflexible attitude about what constitutes Turkish territory brought it to the brink of war with Greece, alienated many of its allies in the wake of action in Cyprus, and is largely responsible for the bloody civil war in the predominantly Kurdish regions of Turkey.

Turkey today is a nation still shaping its identity. It is on the brink of economic growth, on the brink of political stability, on the brink of democracy. And yet, for now, something still holds it back. The dreams of Atatürk remain just that—dreams, haunting his people as they strive toward shaping them into reality.

The creation of the Republic of Turkey at the beginning of the twentieth century was one of the most wondrous transformations in history. Turkey exists today as a testament to the vision of Atatürk. But whether it will move beyond his legacy or become a prisoner of it remains uncertain.

Chronology

1881   Mustafa Kemal is born in Salonica.

1907   The Committee of Union and Progress (C.U.P.) is formed.

1908   Young Turk revolution forces Ottoman sultan to restore the constitution and call for free elections.

1909   C.U.P. military marches on Istanbul after counter-revolution. A new sultan is proclaimed.

1912–1913   The Balkan Wars take place.

1914   World War I begins. Turkey enters war after forming an alliance with Germany.

Timeline

1907
The Committee of Union and Progress (C.U.P) is formed

1912–1913
The Balkan Wars take place

1914
World War I begins. Turkey enters war after forming an alliance with Germany

1923
Treaty of Lausanne is signed. Assembly declares that Turkey is a republic. Mustafa Kemal is elected as its first president. Capital is moved from Istanbul to Ankara

1907   **1928**

1908
Young Turk revolution forces Ottoman sultan to restore the constitution and call for free elections

1920
San Remo Conference is held, and Treaty of Sèvres is signed, dividing the Ottoman Empire

1928
Turkey is officially declared a secular republic. Arabic numbers and alphabet are replaced by the Latin (Western) alphabet and numbers

1915–1916 Mustafa Kemal successfully repels attempted Allied invasion of Gallipoli.

1919 Mustafa Kemal issues "Declaration of Independence" after landing at Samsun.

1920 San Remo Conference is held, and Treaty of Sèvres is signed, dividing the Ottoman Empire.

1921 Name of new state is declared to be Turkey.

1922 Monarchy is abolished in Turkey, and the sultan leaves.

1923 Treaty of Lausanne is signed. Assembly declares that Turkey is a republic. Mustafa Kemal is elected as its first president. Capital is moved from Istanbul to Ankara.

1950
First free and open elections are held. Democratic Party wins

1960
Military overthrows government for the first time

1999
Istanbul mayor Recep Erdoğan is arrested and imprisoned after reciting an Islamic poem at a political rally

2003
Recep Erdoğan, a moderate Islamist, becomes prime minister

1950
2008

1974
Kurdistan Workers' Party (PKK) formed by Abdullah Öcalan. Turkey invades Cyprus

1982
New constitution creates more powerful president, elected for a seven-year term

2007
Abdullah Gül becomes Turkey's first Islamist president

2008
Turkey launches land and air attacks against Kurds in northern Iraq

1924 All members of the Ottoman royal family are expelled from Turkey and the caliphate is abolished. Religious courts and schools are banned.

1925 Turkey adopts the Gregorian (Western) calendar and bans the fez.

1928 Turkey is officially declared a secular (non-religious) republic. Arabic numbers and alphabet are replaced by the Latin (Western) alphabet and numbers.

1935 Law is passed requiring Turkish people to take a last name (surname).

1938 Atatürk dies; he is succeeded by Ismet Inönü.

1946 Turkish Democratic Party is formed.

1950 First free and open elections are held. Democratic Party wins.

1952 Turkey joins the North Atlantic Treaty Organization (NATO).

1959 Turkey applies for membership in the European Economic Community (EEC).

1960 Military overthrows government for the first time.

1971 Military again overthrows government in an attempt to restore law and order.

1974 Kurdistan Workers' Party (PKK) formed by Abdullah Öcalan. Turkey invades Cyprus.

1980 Military again takes over government.

1982 New constitution creates more powerful president, elected for a seven-year term.

1984 PKK launches a series of attacks against Turkish forces.

1993 Süleyman Demirel becomes president and appoints Turkey's first woman prime minister, Tansu Ciller.

1999 Istanbul mayor Recep Erdoğan is arrested and imprisoned after reciting an Islamic poem at a political rally.

2001 Main opposition party, pro-Islamist Virtue Party, is officially banned.

2002 Justice and Development (AK) Party wins a majority of seats in Turkish Parliament.

2003 Recep Erdoğan, a moderate Islamist, becomes prime minister.

2007 Abdullah Gül becomes Turkey's first Islamist president.

2008 Turkey launches land and air attacks against Kurds in northern Iraq.

Bibliography

Armstrong, H.C. *Grey Wolf*. London: Arthur Barker, Ltd., 1933.

Ciment, James. *The Kurds: State and Minority in Turkey, Iraq and Iran*. New York: Facts On File, 1996.

Couloumbis, Theodore A. *The United States, Greece and Turkey: The Troubled Triangle*. New York: Praeger Publishers, 1983.

Fromkin, David. *A Peace to End All Peace*. New York: Avon Books, 1989.

Garber, G.S. *Caravans to Oblivion: The Armenian Genocide, 1915*. New York: John Wiley and Sons, 1996.

Hale, William. *The Political and Economic Development of Modern Turkey*. New York: St. Martin's Press, 1981.

Jackh, Ernest. *The Rising Crescent: Turkey Yesterday, Today and Tomorrow*. New York: Farrar & Rinehart, Inc., 1994.

Kinross, Lord. *Atatürk: The Rebirth of a Nation*. London: Weidenfeld and Nicolson, 1964.

Kinzer, Stephen. *Crescent and Star: Turkey Between Two Worlds*. New York: Farrar, Straus, and Giroux, 2001.

Kramer, Heinz. *A Changing Turkey*. Washington, D.C.: Brookings Institution Press, 2000.

Larrabee, F. Stephen. "Turkey Rediscovers the Middle East." *Foreign Affairs*, July/August 2007.

Lewis, Bernard. *The Emergence of Modern Turkey*. New York: Oxford University Press, 3rd ed., 2002.

Mango, Andrew. *Atatürk*. New York: Overlook Press, 1999.

———. *The Turks Today*. New York: Overlook Press, 2004.

McDowall, David. *A Modern History of the Kurds*. New York: I.B. Tauris, 1996.

O'Ballance, Edgar. *The Kurdish Struggle: 1920–94*. New York: St. Martin's Press, Inc., 1996.

Rustow, Dankwart A. *Turkey: America's Forgotten Ally*. New York: Council on Foreign Relations, 1987.

Tapper, Richard, ed. *Islam in Modern Turkey.* New York: I.B. Tauris, 1991.

Turam, Berna. *Between Islam and the State: The Politics of Engagement.* Stanford, Calif.: Stanford University Press, 2007.

WEB SITES

http://europa.eu

www.bbc.co.uk

www.guardian.co.uk/turkey/

www.nytimes.com

www.turkishdailynews.com.tr

www.un.org

Further Resources

Kinross, Lord. *Atatürk: The Rebirth of a Nation*. London: Weidenfeld and Nicolson, 1964.

Mango, Andrew. *Atatürk*. New York: Overlook Press, 1999.

———. *The Turks Today*. New York: Overlook Press, 2006.

McDowall, David. *A Modern History of the Kurds*. New York: I.B. Tauris, 1996.

Morris, Chris. *The New Turkey: The Quiet Revolution on the Edge of Europe*. London: Granta Books, 2007.

O'Ballance, Edgar. *The Kurdish Struggle*. New York: St. Martin's Press, Inc., 1996.

Pope, Nicole, and Hugh Pope. *Turkey Unveiled*. New York: Overlook Press, 2004.

Web sites

BBC News: Turkey
http://www.bbc.co.uk/topics/turkey

Embassy of the Republic of Turkey
http://turkishembassy.org/

Library of Congress Country Studies: Turkey
http://lcweb2.loc.gov/frd/cs/trtoc.html

National Geographic Music: Turkish Classical
http://worldmusic.nationalgeographic.com/worldmusic/view/page.
basic/genre/content.genre/turkish_classical_797

Republic of Turkey Ministry of Culture and Tourism
http://www.kultur.gov.tr/EN/Default.aspx?17A16AE30572D313D4AF1E
F75F7A79681D9DD78D03148A6E

Turkish Connection (Business, arts, and Turkish culture in the United States)
http://www.turkishconnection.com/index.html

Turkish Daily News
http://turkishdailynews.com.tr/

Picture Credits

Index

About the Contributors

Author **Heather Lehr Wagner** is an editor and writer. She has an M.A. in government from the College of William and Mary and a B.A. in political science from Duke University. She is the author of more than 40 books exploring political and social issues, including several other volumes in the CREATION OF THE MODERN MIDDLE EAST series.

Series editor **Arthur Goldschmidt Jr.** is a retired professor of Middle East History at Penn State University. He has a B.A. in economics from Colby College and M.A. and Ph.D. degrees from Harvard University in history and Middle Eastern Studies. He is the author of *A Concise History of the Middle East*, which has gone through eight editions, and many books, chapters, and articles about Egypt and other Middle Eastern countries. His most recent publication is *A Brief History of Egypt*, published by Facts On File in 2008. He lives in State College, Pennsylvania, with his wife, Louise. They have two grown sons.